WONDER CATS

WONDER CATS

Text contributed by Lucy York.

Summersdale Publishers Ltd
46 West Street
Chichester
West Sussex
PO19 1RP
UK

www.summersdale.com

Printed and bound in Great Britain

ISBN: 978-1-84953-042-2

WONDER CATS

TRUE STORIES OF EXTRAORDINARY FELINES

ASHLEY MORGAN

CONTENTS

ACKNOWLEDGEMENTS

In researching this book I have learned that cat lovers and owners are themselves a breed apart. I would like to say a big thank you to everyone who took the time to share their cats' incredible stories with me: it has been a great pleasure.

Thanks go to Joan Payne for Speedy's story; Anna Levermore for Kizzy's story; to Jessica Ford for Pip's story; to Amanda Crosthwaite for Feet's story; to Jessie Sculpher for Tabitha's story; to John and Sharron Scrupps for Joey's story; to Helen Frankish for Casper's story; to Francesca Robinson for Mia's story; to Audrey Plumpton for Lucky's story; and to Mandy Parsall for Felix's story.

Special thanks go to Zahir White and Louise Waters at Cats Protection – your patience and help is much appreciated.

ACKNOWLEDGEMENTS

INTRODUCTION

Cats have lived alongside humans for thousands of years: in Ancient Egypt they were worshipped as gods; in medieval times they were reviled as demons; in modern times they have become enduringly popular family pets and companions. And yet, though cats have cohabited with humans for centuries, they still have the capacity to astound and surprise us.

Gathered together in this anthology are stories that will truly make you wonder at these versatile, intelligent and resourceful creatures. There are cats with unique abilities, cats that have survived horrific accidents, cats that have embarked on epic journeys, cats that have showed great heroism in times of duress and even cats that have made a name for themselves in their chosen career. Many of the stories have been reported in the media around the world, but there is also a selection of moving first-hand accounts by people whose lives have been touched by these remarkable felines.

Cats are often misrepresented as carefree, independent animals, with little interest in their human companions other than as a source of food and shelter. It's true what they say – you don't own your cat, your cat owns you. But as these stories show, they are capable of great compassion and friendship, and anyone who lives with a cat will surely tell you that they are worth more than their weight in gold.

UNEXPECTED HEROES

Cats are not often given the recognition that dogs receive for saving people's lives; you don't tend to hear dramatic stories of cats leaping to the rescue of a drowning child, for example. Yet cats have nevertheless proved themselves to be capable of heroic actions in times of need, and often in unexpected ways.

Cats' heightened perception means that they are able to sense things that we humans cannot; some of the stories in this section show how cats have used this advantage to save their owners from dangers that they would have otherwise remained blissfully unaware of until it was too late.

Other cats have been able to raise the alarm or go and fetch help when their owner was injured or trapped and in need of help. Without any previous training or prompting from their owner, they seem instinctively to know what to do.

Then there are the cats that are everyday heroes in their selfless devotion to a human that has come to rely on them: cats can give confidence to the socially disadvantaged, provide an early warning system for people who have seizures, or act as the ears and eyes for people who are deprived of those senses.

SIMON

Simon is credited with saving the lives of Royal Navy officers on board the HMS *Amethyst* during the Chinese Civil War in 1949, and is the only cat ever to have been awarded the PDSA's Dickin Medal for bravery...

In 1948 the British frigate HMS *Amethyst* was stationed in Hong Kong. One day crew member George Hickinbottom, just 17 at the time, found an undernourished black and white cat wandering the dockyards. George smuggled the cat, soon to be named Simon, aboard the *Amethyst*, where he set to work catching and killing rats on the lower decks and quickly became popular with the crew – the ship's unofficial lucky mascot.

During a trip up the Yangtze River to Nanking to relieve the HMS *Consort* from duty, the *Amethyst* came under siege from the People's Liberation Army. Later to become known as the Yangtze Incident, the siege lasted for 101 days. Throughout that time, Simon was hard at work killing off rats that had launched their own siege on the ship's food supplies, having gained access to the ship in great numbers as the vessel was moored up in the river. Running out of food supplies could have been catastrophic for the crew – there was no way for them to replenish stocks whilst under siege.

Very early on in the siege Simon suffered severe shrapnel wounds when an onslaught of shelling penetrated the captain's cabin, killing Commander Bernard Skinner. Simon managed to drag himself out of the cabin onto the deck, where he was quickly taken to the ship's medical bay. Medical staff treated his burns and removed four pieces of shrapnel from his wounds – they didn't expect him to last the night. But against all odds he made it through and went straight back to his duties of keeping the rat population under control. He also made regular appearances in the sick bay, helping to raise the morale of wounded sailors, many of whom were just teenagers.

By the time the ship escaped from the river, news of Simon's heroic actions had spread and he'd become somewhat of a celebrity. He was showered with praise at every port the ship called at on the passage back to Britain and received a hero's welcome when the *Amethyst* finally returned to dock in Plymouth on 1 November 1949. Letters from fans and admirers arrived in their thousands – there was such a deluge that he was assigned his own Naval officer to deal with the fan mail.

Though a celebrated hero, Simon still had to go through quarantine on his arrival back in the UK. Sadly, he died there three weeks later at the age of just two from a complication of the viral infection caused by his earlier wounds. A funeral with full military honours was held for him at the PDSA Animal Cemetery in Ilford, Essex. Hundreds attended, including the entire crew of the HMS *Amethyst*. He was posthumously awarded the PDSA Dickin Medal, which is the charity's animal equivalent of the Victoria Cross, and was also recognised with the rank of Able Seaman.

Commander Stuart Hett, speaking at a ceremony in 2007 to commemorate Simon's bravery, said: 'Simon's company and expertise as a rat catcher were invaluable during the months we were held captive. During a terrifying time, he helped boost the morale of many young sailors, some of whom had seen their friends killed. Simon is still remembered with great affection.' The director general of the PDSA, Marilyn Rydström, commented that: 'The power of animals to support and sustain morale in times of conflict can never be underestimated.'

Honouring heroic animals

Simon is the only cat out of 62 animals to have received the PDSA Dickin Medal, an award created by the People's Dispensary for Sick Animals (PDSA) in 1943. Other recipients include 32 World War Two messenger pigeons, three horses and 26 dogs. The Ilford PDSA Animal Cemetery where Simon was buried is the final resting place of around 3,000 animals, of which 12 are PDSA Dickin Medal recipients, so he is in good company.

SPEEDY

When Joan Payne from Aldeburgh, Suffolk, brought home a little tabby named Speedy as a companion for her housebound daughter Christine, she began to realise that a cat doesn't have to do anything dramatic to be a true hero…

Joan's nineteen-year-old daughter Christine suffers from various serious conditions, including progressive spinal ataxia and epilepsy, and has severe learning difficulties. She has extreme difficulty in walking and suffers grand mal seizures. Because of her medical condition, Joan explains, Christine has to spend her life at home.

“*Christie is a very severely handicapped little girl whose whole world is around the home. She is very isolated. We decided to get Christie a cat to help bring some life into her lonely world. We went to the animal rescue centre where there were so many cats to choose from. The lady showed us a very small dainty tabby with delicate features. She seemed very lady-like – I would say she was elegant in how she walked. Her cry was very soft and gentle and she seemed to have a very caring nature.*

We brought her home and she was very nervous. She hid in her bed, only venturing out at night when it was quiet. She did a room at a time, taking it very slowly and settling in to her new surroundings. She eventually found her way to Christie's room where she seemed to settle in very quickly. She soon made herself at home, lying on the arm or the back of Christie's chair and on her bed at night. We even had to bring her biscuits in. When Christie was washed Speedy would sit and wash herself. They seemed to just hit it off – like they both needed someone. ”

Joan was pleased that Speedy and Christine had formed such a strong bond and noticed a real improvement in her daughter, who seemed a lot brighter and happier since Speedy had joined the household. But Speedy's support for Christine went beyond providing comfort and companionship.

“ *One day Speedy seemed very distressed and would not settle. When I looked at Christie I could see she was unwell. So we put her to bed and when Speedy came in to the kitchen crying and clawing I saw Christie was having a fit. We gave Christie her medication and both Speedy and Christie slept. Christie seemed calmer for having Speedy there. We thought how lucky we were that Speedy had noticed because when Christie has grand mal seizures she just suddenly falls.* ”

Since then there have been other occasions when Speedy has predicted that Christine was about to have a seizure. The two-year-old cat has not just changed Christine's life by providing friendship and relief from her loneliness, but also Joan's life by giving her the reassurance of knowing that she's always at her daughter's side, watching over her.

> “*When Speedy cries and claws we know what is going to happen. She is like an alarm clock. Speedy seems to have given up any life of her own to give a lonely little girl a life. She has really changed ours.*”

Speedy is an everyday hero in the Payne household, and in 2008 she was honoured by Cats Protection with a Rescue Cat Award in the Hero Cat category.

Cats Protection

The UK's leading feline welfare charity, Cats Protection, was formed in 1927 by a group of like-minded people led by Jessey Wade who were devoted to promoting the interests of domestic cats. The charity now re-homes and reunites 55,000 cats and kittens every year through their network of over 250 voluntary-run branches and 29 adoption centres. Its vision is a world where every cat is treated with kindness and an understanding of its needs. The organisation also holds the Rescue Cat Awards, in which owners of cats adopted from the charity's rescue centres may nominate their cat for an award in one of the following categories: Hero Cat, Ultimate Survivor, Best Friends and Most Incredible Story.

SYLVESTER

A 90-year-old woman from Rotura, New Zealand, had her loyal cat Sylvester to thank for fetching help when her life was endangered…

Patricia Kerr, aged 90, adopted Sylvester, a ginger, part-Persian stray and by 2007 she had had him for about five years. During that time her neighbours, Shirley and Monte Mason, said he had always refused to be touched by anyone other than his owner and shied away from other people.

So when Sylvester turned up on their doorstep meowing loudly one day, the couple were surprised and concerned, especially as they had thought that Mrs Kerr was at home. Shirley Mason tried calling Mrs Kerr on the phone, but it was engaged so she assumed she was OK. She and her husband had to go to a funeral that day, but when they returned they saw that Mrs Kerr hadn't put out her rubbish for collection – it was highly unusual for her to have forgotten. So they tried the phone again, and this time when it was engaged they tried her door – there was still no response, so they called the police.

The police broke in to find Mrs Kerr trapped in her bath. No one knew how long she had been in there, but the water had gone cold and she was hypothermic. They had got there just in time and the elderly lady recovered from the ordeal after a short stay in hospital. Sylvester was still keeping a customary low profile after the incident, but the Masons credited him with helping to save his owner's life.

TOTO

In Italy in 1944, a cat named Toto astonished his owners and saved their lives by demonstrating a seeming ability to predict the imminent future…

In March 1944 in the village of San Sebastiano al Vesuvio, Gianni and his wife Irma noticed that their two-year-old black cat Toto seemed uneasy and was acting strangely. It took them a long time to entice him indoors at dusk, but eventually they got him inside and went to bed.

Just after midnight, Gianni was woken by Toto clawing at his cheek. Angry at being disturbed in this way, the farmer pushed him away. He was about to eject the cat from the bedroom when his wife intervened. Toto was normally a docile cat, so Irma suspected that something was wrong and that the cat could be trying to warn them of something. She eventually persuaded her husband that they should leave their house. The couple packed up a few things and headed to Irma's sister's house a short distance away.

Within an hour, Mount Vesuvius erupted and sent a river of lava down the mountainside that obliterated San

Sebastiano al Vesuvio and killed 30 people. If it weren't for Toto, that number might have been 32. The neighbouring villages of Massa di Somma, Ottaviano and part of San Giorgio a Cremano were also destroyed in this unexpected and violent eruption.

Whether or not Toto really could predict the future, we cannot know. It is more likely that he was able to sense changes in the environment that preceded the eruption. Cats are thought to be able to detect the presence of positively charged ions in the atmosphere and to sense increases in electrostatic activity, as well as changes in magnetic fields.

WALLACE

One morning in January, Maureen Gorman and her daughter were woken abruptly by their black cat, Wallace; he seemed to be trying to warn them that something was amiss in their home in Carnoustie, Scotland…

Maureen Gorman had adopted Wallace, a five-year-old black cat, from a rescue centre in December. In January, Maureen and her daughter, Pamela, were fast asleep in their home in Carnoustie, Scotland. In the early hours of the morning their rest was disturbed by Wallace. Normally a very quiet cat, Wallace appeared very agitated and was making a lot of noise trying to get Maureen up. She realised something wasn't right, and accompanied him downstairs.

Wallace led her straight to the living room and began scratching at the door. She followed him inside the room, where he made a beeline for the computer. That's when Maureen saw that smoke was billowing out of the back of it. Thinking on her feet, she quickly unplugged the machine and put the fire out before it could spread.

'Wallace must have seen it start to smoulder and come upstairs to warn me,' Maureen explained, 'he was quite the hero! I shudder to think what would have happened if Wallace had not been around.'

Maureen was so impressed by her cat's heroic action that she nominated him for a Cats Protection Rescue Cat Award in 2008 – and he was short-listed as a finalist in the Hero Cat category. 'He's a wonderful cat,' said Maureen, 'he's such a good friend and I would say he is our hero.'

Police in Columbus, Ohio, responded to a 911 call from Gary Rosheisen's address, but were surprised to find a cat waiting for them by the phone when they arrived at the disabled man's apartment…

Gary Rosheisen was wheelchair-bound and suffered from osteoporosis, and occasional mini-strokes that affected his balance. He lived alone in an apartment with his orange-and-tan-striped cat, Tommy, who he had got three years previously to help lower his blood pressure.

One Thursday night Gary fell from his wheelchair, and because of his medical conditions couldn't get himself back up off the floor. Gary had been equipped with a medical alert necklace to contact paramedics in such an emergency, but on this occasion he wasn't wearing it, and there was no way he could reach the emergency chord above his pillow. He was stuck.

Shortly after the time of his fall, the police received a 911 call which they traced back to Gary's apartment – but they couldn't hear anyone on the end of the line. Thinking it might be a misdial, the police called back to check everything was OK. When no one picked up they prepared to go to the apartment and check on the situation.

Arriving at Gary's home, the police were greeted with the sight of a cat lying by the telephone on the living room floor. Then they saw Gary, who was on the ground near his bed.

Gary explained to the police that Tommy must have made the 911 call. Officer Patrick Daugherty, who was at the scene, said, 'I know it sounds kind of weird.' But there wasn't any other possible explanation.

Gary had tried to teach Tommy how to dial 911, but until that day he wasn't sure that his training had sunk in. Gary kept his phone on the living room floor – it had only 12 small buttons, including a speed dial for 911 just above the speaker phone button. So it would have been fairly easy for Tommy to go to the phone and press the right button with his paw when he saw that his owner was in trouble. 'He's my hero,' Gary said.

WINNIE

One night in New Castle, Indiana, the Keeslings' family cat Winnie detected a deadly danger creeping silently into their home…

On 24 March 2007, the Keesling family were fast asleep in bed and unaware that carbon monoxide was leaking from the gasoline-powered water pump in their basement and filling their home. Carbon monoxide is a dangerous odourless gas that causes carbon monoxide poisoning, which can be lethal if not treated quickly.

At about 1 a.m., 14-year-old cat Winnie went into the bedroom where Eric and Cathy Keesling were sleeping and started to jump on the bed, meowing loudly and nudging Cathy's ear. Cathy was slow to get up, but Winnie was very persistent. 'It was a crazy meow,' said Cathy, 'almost like she was screaming.'

It was only when she got up that Cathy realised she felt faint and nauseous. She would start to swoon, only to be revived again by Winnie's incessant caterwauling. When Cathy couldn't wake her husband Eric she decided to call 911 – he had undergone minor neck surgery the day before, so Cathy was worried. But she was so disorientated she found it difficult to dial and was unable to speak.

The call was traced to the Keeslings' home, and when paramedics arrived at the scene they found the couple's 14-year-old son, Michael, passed out on the floor near his bedroom. It looked like they had only just got there in time. The paramedics put oxygen masks on the Keeslings and quickly escorted them out of their home. They were treated for carbon monoxide poisoning and fortunately made a full recovery.

As for Winnie, she was named the hero of the hour, and was later honoured with the title 'Cat of the Year' by The American Society for the Prevention of Cruelty to Animals (ASPCA). She was certainly a special cat – the previous summer, when tornadoes tore through the area, 45 miles east of Indianapolis, Cathy said Winnie had behaved in a similar way. 'I really believe cats can sense these kinds of things,' she said.

TOM 2

Betty Macaluso was deaf and lived alone in her home in Lawrenceville, Georgia. Luckily, she had a four-legged alarm clock and helper in the form of her orange and white cat Tom 2…

Betty Macaluso from Lawrenceville, Georgia, had been deaf all her life, so an alarm clock wouldn't have been much use to her for waking her up in the morning. Instead, she relied on Tom 2, her orange and white cat, and his brother Tiger, a grey and black tabby, to do the job. Every morning at 6 a.m., Tom 2 would gently paw her arm to tell her that it was time to get up and feed him his breakfast.

But Tom 2 wasn't only interested in getting his owner to feed him – he would also let his owner know when someone was at the door or calling on her video phone. Betty, who was in her late sixties, adopted the two cats from PetSmart in Lawrenceville when they were just three months old. Speaking through a sign language interpreter, Betty explained: 'They know I can't hear. They do hear for me.'

One morning, Tom 2 seemed to want to tell Betty something. The cat perched on Betty's stomach as she lay in bed, staring up at an area of the ceiling just above her bed. He kept looking up at the spot at different intervals every day for about a week, so Betty decided to investigate. She shined a torch at the spot on the ceiling that was holding his attention and noticed a thin, round line of clay there. Suspecting that an infestation of some sort might be to blame Betty called pest control, who were able to confirm that she had a termite infestation in her home. The exterminator who examined Betty's property was immediately puzzled as to how Betty had detected the termites – usually the first people know about them is when they hear them moving about, which Betty obviously couldn't have done. Betty proudly pointed to her clever cat. Tom 2's discovery came as no surprise to Betty, as he had always been very sensitive to whatever was going on in the house. 'He notices the smallest things, a spider on the ceiling, an ant crawling on the floor,' Betty elaborated.

Betty's parents were also deaf, and the family had always kept cats at home. One evening when she was a young girl, she was sitting out on the porch swing with her mother when the family cat began behaving in a strange manner. They couldn't work out what had got into him – until they saw him launch an attack on a rattlesnake that lay just five feet away from them. Betty believed that the cat had saved her from being bitten by the rattlesnake. From then on she always lived with cats, so that they could act as her ears.

All ears

Cats have an acute sense of hearing and can detect a very wide range of frequencies. They are able to hear higher pitched sounds than humans and even dogs: anything from 55 Hz up to 79 kHz and 10.5 octaves. Humans' range is restricted to 31 Hz to 18 kHz and 9 octaves, while dogs' hearing ranges from 67 Hz to 44 kHz and 9 octaves. This heightened sense allows cats to hear the ultrasonic calls that many species of rodents make. Their sensitive hearing is further enhanced by their large movable outer ears which help to amplify sounds and enable them to sense the direction from which a noise is coming.

PROTECTING PEOPLE FROM HARM

Cats are naturally territorial creatures, especially tomcats, so it comes as no surprise to hear of a cat fending off an intruder on its home turf. But when that intruder is about ten times the size of the cat in question – well, that raises an eyebrow or two!

In this section we see just how fearless cats can be, whether they are guarding their territory by taking on an opponent much bigger than themselves, or showing their maternal side by protecting their owners or the vulnerable from harm.

SOSA

In Quebec, Canada, a woman was protected from a deadly visitor to her garden by her loyal pet cat…

It was 27 July 2003 and Kimberley was working in her garden in Quebec. Her cat, Sosa, was also out in the garden on this summer's day. Kimberley was concentrating on her work when she suddenly came across an unexpected intruder in her garden – an eastern cottonmouth snake. These reptiles are highly poisonous, and its presence in her garden was very unusual, since the species is not native to the province of Quebec. By the time Kimberley saw the snake it was just inches away and poised, ready to strike.

Luckily for Kimberley, Sosa leaped into action, jumping between her owner and the deadly creature and lashing out at it. The snake was frightened off, but not before it had dealt Sosa a bite on the paw. The cat was rushed to a nearby animal hospital and given urgent treatment. Much to Kimberley's relief, her brave and loyal cat made a full recovery after three days at the clinic.

Kimberley was grateful to Sosa for her quick and selfless action. Since the eastern cottonmouth is not native to Quebec, there would have been no ready supply of antivenin available – meaning that a bite could have proved fatal for Kimberley. In 2004, Sosa was honoured for bravery by being inducted into the Purina Animal Hall of Fame. It was never discovered how the deadly snake had come to be in Kimberley's garden.

JACK

Donna Dickey from West Milford, New Jersey, got a surprise one day when her neighbour called to say that her cat Jack was terrorising a bear...

Ten-year-old ginger tom Jack was a territorial cat that didn't like any animals trespassing in the garden of his owner Donna Dickey's home in West Milford, New Jersey. One morning, neighbour Suzanne Giovanetti was astonished to see that the feisty feline had taken exception to an unusual visitor to the street.

A young black bear had been taking a stroll through the woods and had wandered into Donna's garden. Not to be intimidated by the 15-stone intruder, Jack confronted the bear with a barrage of hissing and spitting, causing it to flee and shoot 50 feet up a nearby tree. The frightened youngster hid up there for fifteen minutes before venturing nervously back down – only to be set upon by Jack again and forced up another tree.

Suzanne managed to get some amazing photographs of the bizarre scene, and then thought it best to let her neighbour Donna know what her ferocious pet was up to. Donna called Jack back into the house, allowing the shaken bear to make a hasty retreat into the woods.

West Milford has a high population of bears, but they won't be paying the Dickey household any more visits if Jack has anything to do with it. Donna Dickey summed the incident up quite simply: 'It's obvious he doesn't want anybody else in his yard.' Bears: beware!

UNNAMED STRAYS

In Argentina, a little boy who was lost on the streets in freezing winter weather was saved by a group of stray cats…

In December 2008, a policewoman named Alicia Lorena Lindgvist was out walking along a canal in the Christ King district of Misiones, Argentina, when she noticed a group of cats huddled around together. Finding it unusual to see such a large number of cats grouped together in this way, she went over to investigate.

That's when she saw the little boy, lying in the midst of the cats in the gutter with scraps of food on the ground around him. He was filthy and the cats were all licking at him, trying to get him clean. 'When I walked over they became really protective and spat at me,' she said. 'They were keeping the boy warm while he slept.'

When admitted to hospital, the boy was estimated to be one year old. The doctors who examined him said that he wouldn't have survived out in the cold if it weren't for the warmth provided by the protective felines. Police managed to track down the boy's father, a homeless man who had lost his son while trawling the streets for cardboard to sell. Officer Lindgvist remarked, 'The cats knew he was fragile and needed protecting.'

Stray or feral?

There are estimated to be some two million stray cats on the streets of the UK.

Feral and domestic cats are of the same species – what distinguishes them is whether or not they have human contact during the critical first few weeks of life. If a pet cat had kittens, and her owners did not handle them, those kittens would be equally nervous and may be described as 'feral'. If 'feral' kittens are not rescued and neutered, they will be capable of breeding at six months old – colonies of feral cats can develop rapidly in this way.

With the right care and attention, cats that have lived as strays can become accustomed to human contact and make loving family pets.

Charities such as the Celia Hammond Animal Trust work hard to control the UK's population of stray cats by neutering, and in some cases relocating or re-homing them. In some areas stray cats are tolerated because they are recognised as a form of rodent control. Sadly, however, there are still organisations that euthanise strays.

RAMSES

While taking a Sunday morning stroll through town in Austin, Texas, the last thing Emma Betts expected was to come face to face with a tiger. But what her Canadian hairless cat Ramses did next was even more surprising…

It was Sunday and filming was in progress for an advertisement for a men's body spray called Tiger Heat, manufactured by a company based in Austin. The highlight of the advert was to be the appearance of Sasha, a trained Siberian tiger.

When the production crew took a break for mid-morning coffee, handler Doug Willis led Sasha back to her holding pen. But Doug had forgotten to fasten the gate. 'I only turned my back for a moment,' he said. 'But that's a tiger for you… quick and stealthy. A moment was all Sasha needed to make her escape.' And escape she did – out of the cage, out of the room and downstairs to the front doors of the building before anyone even noticed that she had gone.

FedEx employee Albert Fatz, who had just arrived with a delivery, certainly wasn't expecting to see a 400-pound tiger exiting the building when he pulled open the door. 'I couldn't believe my eyes,' he said. 'I propped the door open to bring in a dolly full of packages, and here comes this tiger strutting right out the door...'

Out on the street, the usually docile and well-trained Sasha was unnerved by the sudden noise and commotion of the outside world, and went on the defensive. One eyewitness described how the big cat stood and growled at everyone. 'I dove into a trashcan to hide I was so scared.'

It was then that 65-year-old Emma Betts, out for a walk with her cat Ramses, approached the scene. The pair both saw the tiger at the same time, and Emma froze in fear. But Ramses reacted rather differently to the unexpected threat. Leaping from his owner's arms, the hairless cat headed straight towards Sasha.

A group of astonished onlookers watched as the two cats squared off and stared at each other. Suddenly Sasha let out an almighty roar and swiped at Ramses, who quickly dodged out of the way. Rather than fleeing from the attack, the 10-pound cat drew himself up and replied with a 'roar' of his own, baring his teeth and hissing and growling at the big cat. If that wasn't shocking enough, no one could have expected Sasha's reaction: the 'ferocious' tiger turned tail and ran back inside the building.

Inside, Doug eventually managed to track Sasha down and take her back to the holding pen. Disappointingly for the Tiger Heat team, the whole incident meant that Sasha had to be replaced by a digital tiger in the advertisement.

Though shaken by the incident, no harm came to Emma Betts, who said, 'I thank my stars for Ramses. He is truly a hero among cats.' Ramses seemed to take it all in his stride, including being awarded a Medal of Courage.

KITTYBABY

Nancy Strand and her Persian cat Feral lived a quiet life in the Tongass National Forest in south-eastern Alaska. A new addition to the family, a tough-looking stray christened KittyBaby, earned his place at her hearth by providing a special service…

Nancy Strand's cabin in the Tongass National Forest of south-eastern Alaska was in a quiet spot, set against the backdrop of the temperate rainforest and with a beach for a front garden. Nancy and her cat Feral lived a peaceful and solitary life there, so when a rugged-looking stray cat turned up it was something of a surprise. But Nancy couldn't resist taking him in, and the newcomer, named KittyBaby, soon settled in.

There were some other changes going on in the neighbourhood at the time. The local council had begun a recycling and refuse collection service from houses in Nancy's area, and residents had to leave their bags of rubbish outside for pick-up. There were also some new arrivals – around thirty bears that had been moved from the nearest city because they'd made a nuisance of themselves there, rifling through everyone's rubbish. Some of these bears started to pass through Nancy's neighbourhood, on the hunt for their usual meal of refuse scraps.

One evening Nancy was about to pop out when KittyBaby very determinedly came and leaned against her leg, directing her away from the door. When she went outside the following day she realised that a bear had been at her bins during the night. This wasn't the only time that KittyBaby acted in this way – on quite a few occasions he seemed to sense something was outside, and stood between his owner and the door, growling like a guard dog.

KittyBaby kept up his bear-warning services all through the summer. Whenever Nancy came home from work after a nightshift, he would meet her at the end of the path to her cabin – but only if no bears were around. If Nancy didn't see KittyBaby waiting in his usual spot when she pulled up, she would know that a bear was nearby, and would wait safely in the car until her little bodyguard turned up to guide her safely into the house.

UNSHKINS

In Los Angeles, a wheelchair-bound man was marked out by two criminals as an easy target. But they weren't counting on a furious ball of fur named Unshkins jumping to his aid...

Peter Choyce from Los Angeles suffered from a damaged spine, and though he could sometimes manage to get around with a walking stick, he spent most of his time in a wheelchair. He would often spend his afternoons parked up in a neighbour's driveway, enjoying the warm weather while working on his memoir on his laptop, with his cat Unshkins for company.

On one such sunny afternoon he was at work in his usual spot when a white car pulled up. Two men got out of the car, and one of them walked up to Peter. Suddenly, he punched Peter in the face and grabbed the laptop. Before Peter even had chance to register what was happening, Unshkins, until now sitting quietly beneath his chair, flew through the air, claws bared, and launched a frenzied attack on the criminal's face. Bloodied and stunned, the criminal then received a punch square in the throat from Peter.

Peter described his cat Unshkins as somewhat of a cranky and aggressive creature, and thought that she acted out of self-preservation rather than to protect her owner. But either way, if it wasn't for her the thief would have got away with it, and Peter wouldn't have found the strength to fight back. In an adrenalin rush fuelled by Unshkin's brave actions, Peter managed to get out of his chair to pursue the man a little way down the street, who turned and ran back toward his car. Unfortunately, the laptop was dropped and irretrievably damaged during the chase and the two miscreants made off in their car.

Peter said of the incident: 'I think they saw a guy in a wheelchair and figured I would be an easy mark. But in the end, me and Unshkins kicked his ass.'

AGGIE

Lynn and John Seely's pet, Aggie, was a gentle cat that had never scratched anyone, until one night when she sensed danger in their home...

When the Seelys first met Aggie she was a poorly little calico kitten that they took pity on. They took her in with plans to nurse her back to health then find her a new home, but somehow they never did get round to giving her away. Aggie was a smart little character, a very gentle cat, and she soon settled in to their home.

One night the couple were fast asleep with Aggie curled up at their feet. An unusual sound in the house must have woken Aggie, because she crept downstairs and climbed in to her cat tree. A man had broken in to the Seelys' house and was moving stealthily through the darkened rooms. As he passed the cat tree, unaware of Aggie's presence, he was viciously attacked as a blur of fur jumped out of the darkness and clawed his face.

The would-be burglar cried out in shock, waking Lynn and John, who were still sleeping upstairs. But when they entered the room there was nothing to be seen – just an open window and one of his abandoned shoes. The couple put two and two together and realised what had happened. They were amazed by Aggie's quick-thinking bravery – not least because the little cat was completely blind.

Aggie's story was featured on PAX TV's *Miracle Pets* programme in the USA and by the time she was 14 she had become quite a celebrity, with a story running about her in IAMS' magazine – she even has her own website.

EARNING THEIR KEEP

Cats have certainly found ways of making themselves useful to humans over the years, and this section looks at cats that have made their mark in a broad spectrum of careers. Of course there are the mousers that have kept many a factory floor and ship's supply room rodent free, but then there are those that have answered rather more unusual callings. From stationmasters to postmen's cats, and from detectives to aspiring weather reporters, these felines have proved themselves to be nothing if not ambitious, and a versatile force to be reckoned with in today's tough employment market.

RUSIK

Most cats have a nose for fish, but Rusik's exceptional ability to track down illegally poached sturgeon got him a job with the Russian police...

Rusik first became known to the Russian police force when he wandered into one of their checkpoints. The staff couldn't resist feeding the stray kitten with scraps of sturgeon that had been confiscated from smugglers, and he was soon adopted as the checkpoint's cat.

Rusik gained a keen sense of the taste and scent of sturgeon, as he received it for many of his meals at the checkpoint. Sometime later, police at a checkpoint in the Stavropol region, bordering the Caspian Sea, had the idea of using keen-nosed Rusik to help them uncover illegal stashes of sturgeon.

The Caspian region produces about 95 per cent of the world's caviar, and is plagued by smugglers, who come to the area to capture sturgeon and its roe. They then sell the sought-after roe in Moscow and other cities for a huge profit. It is a big concern for the Russian authorities, as unchecked the intensive smuggling could drive the Caspian sturgeon population to extinction.

Rusik proved to have a real flair for his new job – in fact, he was so good at alerting the police to stashes of sturgeon hidden in trucks and other vehicles that he took over the responsibilities of the local sniffer dog. However obscure the smugglers' hiding place was, Rusik was able to sniff it out.

It's not surprising that Rusik was so good at his job – a cat's sense of smell is reportedly more sensitive than a dog's. However, cats rarely have successful careers as sniffer animals because it is very difficult to train a cat and get it to cooperate in the same way as a dog.

Rusik's career came to a sad and sudden end when he was hit by a car driven by smugglers – police didn't rule out the possibility that it was a deliberate hit and run. He would be fondly remembered by the Russian police he had helped on so many occasions, and he had set an important precedent – the police planned to train other cats and use them in the same way.

LUPIN

In Germany, a cat called Lupin showed aspirations of taking up a career as a weather reporter...

Germany's star weatherman Joerg Kachelmann had just started his two-minute forecast after the news one Tuesday when a surprise guest appeared in the studio. It was the coldest night of the year and Joerg was reminding the public to wrap up warm – but viewers at home were distracted from his message by a shadow with an extended tail passing along at the bottom of their television screens.

Much to the amusement of the viewers, Joerg bent to scoop up the fame-hungry feline, and continued with the weather forecast as Lupin purred in his arms. Joerg wasn't sure how the cat had got into the studio, but it seemed to him that the best course of action was to give him some attention: 'I noticed him when he rubbed against my leg and thought people might wonder what was happening. I figured it would be easier to control the cat by picking him up. Cats get annoyed if they feel ignored.'

Lupin was a pet belonging to a member of the weather team who was away at the time – perhaps he had wandered into the studio looking for his owner. At any rate, he seemed quite at ease. He nibbled Joerg's beard and then joined in with the weather report by pointing a paw at the map, as if to indicate where the temperatures were dropping the most. A wry Joerg later commented: 'I know the English have a saying about raining cats and dogs but unfortunately I couldn't make that joke in Germany.'

BEEZLEY

The real Postman Pat has been making his rounds in Lyme Regis, Dorset, with ginger and white cat Beezley perched in the basket of his bike…

Beezley is a confident cat, often to be seen strolling around his neighbourhood in Lyme Regis, Dorset, completely unperturbed by the presence of dogs. Postman Terry Grinter befriended the six-year-old cat one summer. 'I'm a cat lover so I always used to stroke him,' Terry explained. One day the idea struck him to lift him into the basket on the front of the bike he used to make his rounds. 'I expected him to jump straight out,' he said, but Beezley seemed quite comfortable there.

Soon the fluffy ginger and white tomcat was hopping into Terry's basket of his own accord, accompanying the postman on his rounds at least once or twice a week (if the weather was good) and earning Terry the title of the real Postman Pat. The six-year-old cat rides around perched quite comfortably in the basket and is oblivious to passing traffic – a few times he has even fallen asleep on top of the mailbag, and given Terry a bit of a nip when he had to disturb the snoozing feline to get to the letters he was delivering.

The pair have become a familiar sight in the area, and Beezley enjoys the fuss that's made of him. 'People have said, "Don't tell me he's called Jess," because of Postman Pat's cat, and I have to explain that he's not even mine,' Terry explained. Beezley's owner is Peter Ward, who decided to get a cat to deal with a rat problem in his kitchen. He was planning to get a two-year-old cat with experience of hunting, but when he was presented with a tiny kitten, he couldn't resist adopting Beezley. Though he enjoys his adventures with Terry, Beezley is a loyal cat; whenever the pair cycle past his home, he jumps out of the basket and trots back to his owner.

TIZER

Mice at King's Cross railway station in London have nowhere to hide thanks to the efforts of British Transport Police recruit Tizer…

Thirteen-year-old cat Tizer was adopted by the British Transport Police (BTP) from a rescue centre run by the charity Cats Protection, then inducted into the ranks as an honorary constable. His role of Chief Mouser at King's Cross railway station is an important one – it is his sole responsibility to keep the busy station rodent-free.

Before Tizer came to work at the station, it was overrun with mice, and the BTP were spending vast amounts of money on pest control solutions, with little or no results. But since Tizer has been on the case, the station has become a mouse-free zone.

Tizer shares an office with Inspector Roy Sloane, who adopted him from the rescue centre and signed him up for service. Along with his mouse-catching duties, Tizer has quickly begun to play a valuable role in helping officers to wind down after a stressful day and boosting their morale. He is a playful cat that loves playing fetch with his toy spider, and enjoys being around people. 'Everyone is always asking after him, and he is probably the most popular member of staff,' said the inspector.

It's a good career for a cat

Cats' excellent hunting skills have always found them welcomed into the role of rodent population controllers by humans through the ages – and some of them have made quite a career out of it.

Towser was a tabby that worked as mouse-catcher in a Scotch distillery's grain stores and is said to have caught over 23,000 mice in her 23-year-long career there.

Minnie was the resident rat-catcher at a sports stadium in London, and caught an average of 2,000 rats a year over the six years she worked there.

During World War Two, the British Ministry of Supply put out a request for members of the public to volunteer their pet cats for service. Hundreds of cats were sent in by patriotic owners and were put to the task of keeping army stores vermin free.

FRED

Fred the Undercover Kitty from New York became famous for helping the NYPD to arrest a man suspected of posing as a vet…

Fred was born in the spring of 2005 in Brooklyn, New York. He and sibling George were named after the twins

Fred and George Weasley of *Harry Potter* fame. Just a few months later Fred was rescued by Animal Care and Control of New York City; he was suffering from severe pneumonia and a collapsed lung. An assistant district attorney, Carol Moran, adopted Fred through Animal Care and Control's foster programme, and nursed him back to health. Though he came from an unremarkable background, Fred's adoption by a member of the justice system was the first step on his path to fame.

In February 2006, the Brooklyn District Attorney's office signed up Fred as a secret undercover agent. His mission would be to pose as a would-be patient in an NYPD investigation that sought to apprehend Steven Vassall, who was suspected of illegally working as a vet without a proper licence or training.

On 3 February 2006, Fred took part in a sting operation. Working alongside undercover detective Stephanie Green-Jones, Fred was used as bait to expose Steven Vassall. The man was successfully arrested and later charged with unauthorised veterinary practice, criminal mischief, injuring animals and petty larceny.

In recognition of his contribution to keeping New York's pet population safe from the unqualified medical meddler, Fred was presented with a Law Enforcement Appreciation Award by Brooklyn district attorney Charles J. Hynes on 18 May 2006. He was also honoured later that year in a charity benefit hosted by the New York City Theater District and was presented with the Mayor's Alliance Award, which is given to remarkable animals.

Fred's career moved in a different direction after the Steven Vassall arrest, and he went into training as a therapy animal; eventually he would be taken into classrooms to help teach children how to treat and care for animals.

Fred had become a minor celebrity thanks to his efforts to help fight crime, and owner Carol Moran received many offers from animal talent agencies who wanted to sign up Fred to feature in television commercials. Sadly, the brave cat died in August 2006 at the age of just 15 months when he was hit by a car.

U-BOAT

U-boat was a ship's cat aboard Royal Navy vessel HMS *Snowflake* in World War Two with an uncanny sense of timing...

The HMS *Snowflake* was a 'Flower' class corvette in the British Royal Navy that was sent on convoy duties across the Atlantic during World War Two. At that time, before animals were banned from being onboard Royal Navy vessels in 1975, it was quite common for ships to have a cat. They often came in useful by keeping the rat population down and were considered lucky. None of the crew knew where little U-boat turned up from or how he came aboard, but he was welcomed as their unofficial mascot.

U-boat would cause great amusement amongst the crew when the warning 'action stations' was called by scurrying over to the flour bin in the galley and staying up there until the action was over. When HMS *Snowflake* docked after voyages, U-boat would go on 'shore leave'. Somehow the cat seemed to know when the ship was about to set sail again and would reappear on the dock just in time to jump aboard.

On one occasion, though, there was no sign of U-boat and the crew were running out of time – it looked as though HMS *Snowflake* would have to cast off without him. Many of the crew were alarmed at the thought and threatened to abandon ship – it was considered very bad luck to begin a voyage without the ship's mascot on board. But just as the ship began to ease its way out off from its mooring a blur of grey fur came flying down the jetty at breakneck speed and made a spectacular leap across the widening gap of several feet between the ship and dry land. He landed squarely on the deck to the applause of the crew, then proceeded to do what cats do best – he sat down and gave himself a good wash.

Ships' cats

Cats have a longstanding relationship with seafaring folk throughout history, usually as resident rat-catchers. Many sailors also believed them to bring luck, and ships' cats were sometimes treated as true crew members.

Sailors aboard the *Hecate* even entered their cat Fred Wunpound's name on a census form, and were somewhat put out when his right to vote was refused. The cat served as official mouse-catcher aboard the ship from 1966 to 1974.

The ship's cat aboard the *Liberty* was faithful to his vessel until the last. When the ship ran aground off Cornwall in 1952, he refused to abandon ship and remained onboard for six weeks until he was captured and removed by salvage workers. He was later named Carlsen, after the captain who had refused to leave the sinking US ship *SS Flying Enterprise*.

Siamese cat Princess Truban Tao-Tai had lived aboard the *Sagamore* for 16 years when its owners decided to sell, and was such a part of the furniture that she was listed amongst the fixtures and fittings. The prospective owners weren't sure about keeping the cat at first, but the original owners insisted that she stay – how could she be expected to adapt to life elsewhere after growing up on the ship? In the end a clause was written into the sale contract, stating that the new owners must keep the cat aboard the ship and ensure her happiness until the end of her natural life.

MIKE

A cat named Mike that helped guard the gates of the British Museum in London throughout his life was described as possibly the most famous British cat of the twentieth century…

Mike lived from February 1909 to January 1929 and became famous for guarding the entrance to the British Museum in London for the 20 years of his life.

As a kitten, Mike learned from the British Museum's house cat how to stalk pigeons that had got onto museum property and bring them to the housekeeper in exchange for a tasty treat, before the housekeeper released the pigeons outside the grounds unharmed.

Mike wasn't what you would call a ladies' cat – in fact, he would shun female visitors to the museum. He also had a strong dislike for dogs and was very particular about who was allowed to feed him. As he grew older, only the official gatekeeper and Sir Ernest A. Wallis Budge were allowed this privilege.

When Mike's long and successful life ended, *Time* magazine devoted two articles to him and Sir Wallis Budge wrote an obituary which appeared in the *Evening Standard*. A tombstone was erected near the Great Russell Street entrance to the museum with an inscription that reads: 'He assisted in keeping the main gate of the British Museum from February 1909 to January 1929.'

TAMA

A calico cat named Tama has carved out a career for herself in the field of transportation, working as stationmaster at Kishi Station in Kinokawa, Wakayama Prefecture, Japan…

In April 2006, the Wakayama Electric Railway Company in Japan made all of the stations on its Kishigawa Line unmanned in an effort to reduce spending. The position of stationmaster at each station was to be assigned to a local business employee. A grocer named Toshiko Koyama was made the stationmaster for Kishi station. Little did he know when he was appointed that he was to be ousted from the position by his own cat.

Koyama had adopted several stray cats, which he fed at the station. One of them, a calico cat named Tama, was singled out by railway officials in January 2007 and appointed the official stationmaster. Her primary duty would be to greet passengers at the entrance to the station, and she was kitted out with a stationmaster's hat. Her salary would come in the form of cat food, provided by the railway company.

After Tama took up the role, the publicity generated by the unusual stationmaster led to a sharp increase in passengers using the service. In fact, a study estimated that Tama's presence at the station has helped raise something in the region of 1.1 billion yen in the local economy. The

Wakayama Electric Railway Co said: 'She is the perfect stationmaster. She never complains, even though passengers touch her all over. She has patience and charisma.' Tama's story would seem to prove the old Japanese belief that cats bring in business.

In recognition of her contribution to the business and to the local community, in January 2008 Tama was promoted to 'super stationmaster' and a ceremony attended by the president of the company and the mayor was held to celebrate her success. Her promotion meant that she had become the only female in a managerial position within the railway company. To mark her new position, a ticket booth was equipped with a litter box so that she could have her own 'office'.

Tama also has two feline assistant stationmasters, named Chibi and Miiko. She has featured in a French documentary about cats, *La Voie du Chat*, and a German film called *Katzenlektionen*. Then, in spring 2009, the Kishigawa Line launched its new 'Tama Densha' train, which featured cartoon depictions of the famous Tama. It seems that Tama is well on her way to taking over the world!

SAVING OTHER ANIMALS

Female cats are naturally very protective of their young, but in this section there are tear-jerking examples of how some cats are prepared to go to extremes and risk life and limb for their youngsters.

More surprising, perhaps, are those stories that tell of a cat's efforts to save the life of some other creature that is not part of its immediate family. These examples highlight cats' capacity to be instinctively aware of another living creature's distress and to treat it with the gentle care and compassion they might show their own offspring.

FAITH

When St Augustine's Church in London was hit in an air raid during World War Two, a brave little tabby named Faith stayed to protect her kitten, even as the building collapsed around her...

Faith first arrived at St Augustine's Church as a stray, looking for food and warmth. She was turned out three times by the verger, but when the rector, Henry Ross, saw her he took pity. When nobody came to claim the cat Ross decided to keep her as the church's cat, and named her Faith. She became a popular feature of church services, lying stretched out at Ross's feet or on the front pew during the sermons.

In August 1940, the parish welcomed another new arrival into the fold when Faith gave birth to a black and white tom kitten, named Panda after London Zoo's well-known panda bear Chi-Chi. The two were settled into a basket in the rector's living quarters and getting on very well when Faith began to behave strangely, investigating the different rooms of the house and appearing very restless. One day she took the kitten by the scruff of its neck and moved it down to the basement. When Ross found them there he moved the kitten back upstairs where it was warm. But the next day Faith had moved Panda back to the basement. This happened three times, until Ross gave in and decided to respect Faith's wishes by moving the basket down to the basement, where the pair happily settled in between stacks of music sheets.

On 9 September, Ross had to go to Westminster on business. As he made his way home that evening, the air raid warning was given and he had to spend the night in a shelter. That night the bombing was very severe, and many buildings were destroyed, including eight churches. When he returned home, only the tower of St Augustine's was still standing – his home had been reduced to a mass of rubble, some of which was still on fire. Firemen warned him to move away from the scene, telling him that no one could have survived the blast, but the resolute Ross approached the debris anyway, still holding out hope for his beloved cats.

A faint meowing sound came from beneath a pile of rubble and timbers. Ross struggled to move the debris aside, eventually revealing two dirty, bedraggled, frightened but completely unharmed cats. Relieved and thankful, Ross took the two cats to the safety of the church vestry, which remained intact.

Faith's astonishing story was reported in the papers, and as the news spread many tributes came in. As a civilian cat Faith was not eligible to receive the PDSA's Dickin Medal, an honour reserved for military animals, but founder of the award Maria Dickin did present her with a silver medal in recognition of her steadfast courage. She was the first cat to receive such an accolade for bravery.

Perhaps some would argue that what Faith did is not so extraordinary – after all, it is a natural instinct for a cat to protect her young. But at a time when Britain was under attack and hundreds of people had died in air raids, or had lost their homes, the story of this brave little creature and her kitten surviving against all odds would have brought hope, not just to the local community that had seen its church destroyed, but to the many others who heard her story as it spread through the land.

SCARLETT

A brave mother cat named Scarlett went back into a burning building in Brooklyn five times to rescue each of her kittens from the blaze…

A family of stray cats that had set up home in an abandoned building in Brooklyn had to make an emergency evacuation when the building caught fire. The mother cat (later named Scarlett because of the red patches burned into her fur) carried each of her five four-week-old kittens one by one to safety, returning into the blaze for each one despite her injuries. Her paws were burned and her coat badly singed after the ordeal: when she got all the kittens to safety she performed a headcount by touching each kitten in turn with her nose because her eyes were sealed shut with blisters.

Firefighter and animal lover David Giannelli, who watched the dramatic rescue unfold, took the family to an animal shelter. One kitten was very weak from smoke inhalation and sadly died from a virus, but the rest of the family recuperated together at the animal clinic.

Three months later the cats were all doing well, and the North Shore Animal League had received hundreds of letters from people who had heard or read about Scarlett's amazing story on the news and wanted to adopt her and the kittens. A committee picked three families, two of which were happy to give a home to a pair of kittens each; Oreo and Smokey went to Debbie Palmarozzo in Long Island, while the inseparable Samsara and Panuki went to live with a couple in Port Washington, Long Island.

Scarlett was joyfully received by her new owner Karen, who had lost her own cat seven years before after she had been injured in a car accident. Karen explained: 'The physical and emotional pain I suffered made me more compassionate, and I vowed if ever allowed another cat in my home, it would be one with special needs.'

PUSS PUSS

A gardening job in Cheltenhem turned into a dramatic rescue for Adrian Bunton and Karen Lewis when their cat Puss Puss discovered a distressed lamb in the swimming pool…

In 2003, Adrian Bunton and Karen Lewis, both gardeners, were working in the garden of Cotswold District Council chairman Tim Royle in Icomb, Cheltenham. They had taken their black and white cat Puss Puss along with them for the day.

As they worked, they were suddenly distracted by Puss Puss running to them and meowing frantically, then darting over to the swimming pool and back again. Jill Royle later said, 'She was in a very, very agitated state, meowing and calling and crying and being an utter pest and dashing back and forward...'

Eventually the pair went over to see what all the fuss was about, and saw a lamb trapped under the pool cover, with his head caught up in the cover's straps; they were the only thing keeping him from sinking and drowning. Adrian and Karen guessed that he must have escaped from a pasture nearby and fallen into the pool.

While Adrian jumped into the pool to fish the lamb out, Karen rushed off to get help. Thanks to Puss Puss's fast action, the lucky lamb was saved and made a full recovery.

Karen and Adrian called Puss Puss 'a real little superstar' for saving the day. They were especially proud of her because she is disabled. 'As a kitten she had an accident and had to have her tail amputated,' explained Karen. 'She hasn't grown properly, has arthritis and can't curl up, jump or climb like other normal cats.'

The story appeared in the village newsletter, with the following words from Jill Royle: 'If you see a little black cat with no tail walking in Icomb, it will be gallant Puss Puss, who deserves a medal.'

Making purr-fect sense

Cat owners soon become familiar with their feline friends' vocalisations – and with some cats it seems like there is a different 'meow' for every occasion. But new research has revealed that cats may be using their voices to manipulate their owners for attention or food. Dr Karen McComb at the University of Sussex has identified what she refers to as a 'soliciting purr'. Unlike normal purring, this variety incorporates a 'cry', with a similar frequency to that of a human baby. And that makes it a sound that's very difficult for us humans to ignore. Dr McComb's research was inspired by her own cat, Pepo. 'He would wake me up in the morning with this insistent purr that was really rather annoying.' She discovered that other cat owners experienced the same thing, and when she played the purrs back to people who were not used to spending time with cats, even they found them compelling. Dr McComb believes that cats can learn to exaggerate this particular sound when they realise it's having the desired effect on their owners.

SPARTACUS

Claire Headon from Worthing, West Sussex, was woken one night by her cat Spartacus, who seemed to be trying to tell her something…

Claire had only had ginger tabby Spartacus for three days when her other cat, a black cat named Tori, became ill. Spartacus was sleeping on the end of the bed that night, and woke Claire up at two o'clock in the morning. Claire put on the light and went with him to check on Tori, only to find the black cat had collapsed. The little cat's heart was about to give out.

That's when Spartacus sprang into action; he started biting Tori's neck and pushing her head up. He kept up his efforts to revive the other cat for half an hour, giving Claire time to get dressed and rush Tori to the vet. The vet said that Tori was lucky to be alive, because she should have been dead half an hour ago. Thanks to Spartacus' quick-thinking action, Claire was able to get Tori to the vet in time to save her life. Ever since, Spartacus has followed Tori around and become her bodyguard and protector.

Spartacus has had some other unusual experiences: during the tornado in Birmingham in 2005 he weathered the storm out under a double bed and escaped with just a scratch on his nose; he also once went missing for 46 days, surviving on rainwater – he had lost half his body weight when he returned home. For Claire, though, his most memorable act was saving the life of her other cat, Tori, and for that she calls him her hero. Claire nominated Spartacus for a Rescue Cat Award in 2008, organised by Cats Protection, and he was one of just four finalists in the Hero Cat category.

SUNDAE

When the Church family dog Tiki got into a dangerous predicament in a park in Aurora, Colorado, they were lucky that their cat Sundae was around to raise the alarm…

One Sunday, Lori Church took her two dogs down to Iowa Elementary School's grounds to play. They had been there many times before as the Churches only lived a few doors away and the two family cats tagged along. But on that day, one of the family dogs, named Tiki, mysteriously disappeared.

It was then that one of the two cats, Sundae, began to behave strangely, coming up to her owner and yowling persistently to get her attention. The little cat led Lori about a hundred yards back to an area of the park where they had been sitting a little while before. There Lori saw the opening of a pipe. Sundae went in a few steps, and Lori could hear Tiki way back inside. 'I never would have known that he was in there at all if it hadn't been for the cat,' Lori explained.

There followed a difficult rescue operation involving neighbours, the water department, school security officers and eventually the Aurora firefighters. Poor Tiki had been stuck inside the pipe for eight hours by the time he was pulled out. Sundae stood by watching for three hours, until

Lori took her and the other pets home, then she mounted a vigil from the driveway until Tiki was brought safely home. Lori said that Sundae was ‘as much of a hero as the Aurora Fire Department’.

CARING FOR PEOPLE

The benefit of spending time with cats and other domestic animals has been well documented, with many doctors and specialists believing that it can have a positive effect on blood pressure, heart rate and can help relieve stress.

The number of 'therapy' cats – cats that are trained to provide support and comfort to the unwell – is on the rise, with organisations in both the UK and the US conducting programmes that take the therapy cats out to visit patients in hospitals and care homes. The presence of a cat can help a patient who has become withdrawn to come out of themselves, and elderly patients benefit from working with cats because it gets them thinking about the pets they've had, and so can help improve memory.

But it would seem that cats don't have to be specifically trained to take on a supportive role – many of the stories in this section are about cats that have instinctively and loyally provided their owners with support and care in their times of need. Some cats also seem able to sense illnesses in humans, and to provide an early warning to their owners.

KIZZY

Anna Levermore from Sittingbourne in Kent was diagnosed with Asperger's syndrome when she was seven years old. The condition meant Anna found it hard to fit in, and until she was a teenager she was very lonely. But when she made a new four-legged friend, her life began to change for the better…

" *Kizzy came to us when I was sixteen years old. I pleaded and pleaded with my dad to get a kitten or a young cat. Although both my parents grew up with pets, my dad was against it, saying it might be too traumatic for a kitten to live with a family like us. You see, I wasn't your typical teenager – I was living with a condition called Asperger's syndrome which is a mild form of autism, a neurological developmental condition. This meant making friends was hard, understanding how people felt and at the time trying to control my bad "tantrums" was extremely difficult for me. I was also very lonely and depressed and I didn't have many friends to hang out with like most teenagers of that age do.*

It was when we visited Malta that everything changed. Every evening my family [me, mum, dad and my older brother] would go to the quay to eat dinner. I loved it there because I could sit and stroke a few of the friendly cats and feel happy and relaxed. When we got home, that summer, dad announced we'd pick out a kitten from the local cat rescue centre. I was so excited because I could pick out a cat of my choice and call it what I wanted. My brother wanted to call it 'Spud' but I recoiled at the thought of shouting it's name down the garden to call it in for tea! We choose a cage with some kittens inside of various ages. I wanted a ginger one but it was nasty to my dad. There was a silver tabby that had a cold so we were advised not to choose her. Then this shy, nervous kitten came up to me and I decided to get her. I didn't choose her, she chose me. She was called Jessica but we changed her name to Kizzy as we new she would be no ordinary cat!

So we welcomed a three-month old kitten to our family. Kizzy is now eight years old and she is a calico which means she has a splattering of orange, black and white in her fur. She is a tiny cat and loves to play with her 'one-eared mouse' or 'hamster' toy. Another favourite pastime of hers is to sleep on top of the fish tank lid where it's nice and warm. ”

Kizzy soon settled into the Levermore's home. After she had been there for a while the bond between Kizzy and Anna grew strong and the family started to notice a change in Anna.

"*I never realised Kizzy would help me but she did. I used to be terribly bullied every day of school and was called a "loner". I would come home to be greeted by a polite meow and she would perch on my legs for a cuddle as I went on the computer to relax. She was like the friend I never had. I'd been having tantrums from when I was diagnosed at seven – it was hard for my parents as they found it difficult to cope with my demands as I grew older. Then suddenly when I was seventeen I stopped having them. My family and I believe it is down to the cat. If I had one, Kizzy would get upset and hide under the table or want to be put outside. Seeing her like this made me realise that my tantrums were upsetting her so I started to be a lot calmer around her. She really makes me happy and I like it when she purrs or sleeps with her paw over one eye. Sometimes she'll want to spend lots of time on my lap and sometimes she just wants to sit and listen to me talk or sing to her. I like talking to Kizzy because she is non-judgmental and never answers back. If I upset her she always forgives me with a little dance around my legs. She has helped me find my fiancée by giving me more confidence in myself and helping me to understand that there is life out there. I would recommend anyone with the same condition as me to consider a cat. They could change your life too!*"

In 2008 Kizzy was recognised for her friendship and support when she received a Rescue Cat Award from Cats

Protection in the Best Friends category. Anna says that she doesn't know what she would do without her.

> “*Kizzy has made such a difference to my life. Amazing for a lump of fur on four legs!*”

TEE CEE

Epileptic Michael Edmonds took in a rescue cat that had been dumped in a river as a kitten. Tee Cee, as the new family member was named, soon made himself indispensable to his owner by acting as an early warning system for seizures…

Michael Edmonds from Sheffield had complex epilepsy, meaning that he could suffer violent and dangerous seizures without warning. Rescue cat Tee Cee, a black and white cat that had been dumped in a river as a kitten and brought to a Cats Protection rescue centre, brought reassurance to the family when he proved to have a special skill for predicting Michael's fits.

When Michael is about to succumb to an epileptic fit, Tee Cee sits close to him and stares at his face. ‘When he first did it I thought it was a one-off,’ said Michael, ‘but ever since then he just seems to know.’

Michael's stepdaughter, Samantha Laidler, said that Tee Cee had become a lifeline to her stepfather. Michael's condition had been a constant worry to the family; he was unable to go out on his own, and they were even concerned about leaving him alone in a room for too long. Now they can relax a little bit, because they at least have some warning from Tee Cee, who runs to let Michael's wife know when her husband is having a seizure. 'Once assistance arrives, Tee Cee doesn't leave Michael's side until he regains consciousness and his warnings have proved invaluable to the family,' explained Samantha.

In 2006, Tee Cee was shortlisted for the Hero Cat category at the Rescue Cat Awards 2006, organised by Cats Protection.

Seizure warning system

Research has shown that dogs and cats are able to detect the early warning signs of the onset of a seizure in humans. Some scientists have suggested that the electrical activity that leads to a seizure begins in the brain up to an hour and a half before the patient demonstrates any outward signs. This activity is thought to take place in the part of the brain that regulates heartbeat and perspiration. With their acute sense of smell, both cats and dogs would be able to detect these changes. According to the Epilepsy Foundation, up to ten per cent of dogs appear able to recognise signs of a seizure minutes or hours before the event occurs, and they can be trained to detect the signs and give warning.

Cats are also thought to have this ability but are not used as service animals because they do not respond as well to the necessary training and cannot be relied upon to perform assistance tasks like a dog would.

ANNIE

A cat abandoned by her owner at the Discovery Bay Veterinary Clinic soon found her place as a valuable member of staff…

On a typically busy day at the Discovery Bay Veterinary Clinic in California, a blonde woman walked into the reception area, placed a cat carrier on the floor, and quietly slipped away before any of the preoccupied staff in the hectic clinic noticed. When they examined the carrier, they found a note attached which read 'I am good with children and dogs', and inside the carrier was a calico cat.

An animal control officer was called to remove the cat, but before they arrived the little moggy had won the hearts of the staff and they decided to keep her at the clinic. She was christened 'Orphan Annie' and was inducted as part of the staff team with important duties and special titles of her own: she was made the Greet Cat, Spokes Cat and Hostess with the Mostest for the clinic.

While Annie would spend most of her time sleeping on a chair in the reception area, looking out the window, posing for photographs or greeting new patients as they arrived, she soon proved she was more than just a pretty face; she was unusually sensitive and perceptive in her reactions to situations.

On one occasion a woman who had brought in her very poorly elderly cat was standing at the reception desk in a distressed state, crying quietly to herself. Little Annie had been sleeping comfortably on her usual chair until the woman came in, but as soon as she started crying, Annie leapt to her feet, trotted over and jumped up on to the counter, where she proceeded to purr and rub her face on the sad lady's cheek. This unexpected demonstration of affection soon had the upset woman wiping her tears and cuddling the little calico cat. Since then Annie has provided support and reassurance to many other visitors to the clinic.

It's a sad fact that over four million abandoned cats and captured feral cats are euthanised in shelters in the US every year. Annie was lucky; that her previous owner at least cared enough to bring her in to a veterinary clinic, and that the caring staff were able to keep her on. At six years old she was certainly no longer a kitten – and older cats are usually the hardest to re-home. Happily, Annie was welcomed into a new home where she could make a difference every day by comforting patients and owners visiting the clinic. Not only that: she is a poster child for the abandoned cats of the world and living proof that every cat has something valuable to share.

SEGER

Cindy Herzberg's insightful cat Seger was on the ball when it came to keeping her owner's health in check…

Cindy Herzberg of Canton, Michigan, had a nine-year-old cat named Seger after the musician, Bob. She was an affectionate cat that liked to give her owner lots of attention and had a particular liking for rubbing up against Cindy's neck. But when this habit turned into more of an obsession, Cindy started to think that something wasn't quite right about her cat's behaviour.

'She became very insistent, to the point that it was starting to hurt. She just wouldn't leave my neck alone. After a while, I was wondering what she was trying to tell me, so I went to the doctor,' Cindy explained. After an examination, Cindy was stunned to discover that she had papillary cancer of the thyroid. Aged 45, Cindy had multiple sclerosis and was in a wheelchair but hadn't suffered any unusual symptoms. Cindy described to the doctors what her cat had been doing, and they were more than a little impressed. 'The doctors said Seger was alerting me that something had changed,' said Cindy. 'She was offered a job at the surgeon's office!'

Seger had prompted Cindy to seek medical help for a disease she didn't even know she had before it was too late to treat it. As if that wasn't enough, a few years later Seger gave Cindy another timely warning. 'In the middle of the night she would start hurling herself onto my chest,' Cindy recounted, and this time it didn't take her long to put two and two together. 'I said, "something's not right here, what is she trying to tell me?"'

Once again, Seger had put her paw right on the problem. Cindy went to the doctor and was diagnosed with sleep apnoea, a dangerous condition which causes the sufferer to stop breathing during sleep. It was the experts at the sleep centre's turn to be impressed, and Seger received another job offer from them, which she of course turned down to stay with her owner so she could keep an eye on her. 'This cat could be making all kinds of money. Beyond a shadow of a doubt, she saved my life.'

Is my cat trying to tell me something?

Many people readily accept the ability of dogs to detect illnesses in humans. Medical studies have shown that patterns of biochemical markers have been found in the exhaled breath of patients; with their heightened olfactory sense, dogs may well be able to distinguish these markers and identify the presence of cancer. It is highly possible that cats too are able to detect such things; however, a cat's reaction to such a change may tend to be more subtle than a dog's, so the signals from a cat might be missed. People who are in tune with their cats are more likely to notice behaviour changes, as Cindy did, and act on those signals.

PIP

Jessica Ford from Salisbury, Wiltshire, was diagnosed with acute lymphoblastic leukaemia at the age of 18. One of the things that worried her was how people would react to her changed appearance when she left hospital. But her special friend Pip, a black and white cat that had been her pet since childhood, gave her the confidence to hold her head up high…

" *I was given Pip on my sixth birthday. She was a complete surprise and the best gift I have ever been given still to this day. I have two brothers who are a little older than me and so Pip soon became my number one playmate. She was great fun and I loved caring for her from the outset.*

She was a typical kitten, loving to play and explore the big wide world. I shall never forget the time she bought in her first catch to show me and my family… a crust of bread that Mum had put out for the birds! It was so funny watching her stalk it and pounce, and then to see how proud she was of it as she dropped it on our floor! "

Pip and Jessica became firm friends, and had lots of fun as they grew up together. But when Jess got older, the pair were to be separated for a long period of time and the strength of their friendship tested.

> *In February 2007, when I was 18, I was diagnosed with acute lymphoblastic leukaemia. This would definitely mean in-patient treatment for a number of weeks. Two weeks into my treatment, however, I developed an infection which took me to intensive care and left me unable to move from my bed for the following couple of months. This meant I couldn't go home even for day visits. I started to worry that Pip would forget me in my absence, and as I had lost my hair and a lot of weight I was unsure she would even recognise me.*
>
> *When I was eventually allowed home for a day visit my worries were proved unfounded. She recognised me instantly, running down the garden path to greet me. I was so worried how people would react to me as I looked so different, but she gave me so much confidence in myself and made me realise that even though I didn't look anything like me, I was still the same person. This realisation helped me a lot when dealing with what was happening in my life. She had such a calming effect on me.*

Reassured by Pip's reception on her visit home, Jess returned to hospital to complete the remaining weeks of her treatment.

"*It was a few weeks later that I was allowed to become an out-patient, and it was at this time that Pip helped me more than at any other. Even though I was surrounded by an amazing family, my friends were busy during the day doing their A levels. Pip was an amazing companion, having the ability to make me laugh on good and bad days. That was so important at the time.*

She has always been a very loving cat, sitting on our laps and so on, and this continued. Some days, however, I would be in too much pain for her to sit on me. It was like she had a sixth sense; on the days that I was really bad she wouldn't even attempt to get up on me, she would just stay nearby the whole time. She would sit and wait outside the bathroom whilst I showered, and purr constantly when I came back from my hospital appointments."

In 2008, Jess nominated her constant friend and companion for a Rescue Cat Award organised by the charity Cats Protection, and Pip was selected as a finalist in the Best Friends category.

"*She truly gave me so much courage and the desire to fight on. She was such a relaxing influence on me when I needed to go in for further treatment and having her devoted companionship supported me in ways that a human could not. I loved her so much anyway, but due to the way she acted and responded to me during the worst years of my life I will never forget what an amazingly special cat she is. She is my best friend in the whole world.* ”

STRUIE AND MEALLIE

Struie and Meallie from Inverness were two rescue cats that provided a huge source of comfort and joy to their owner Rhoda McVey's parents during their final years of life...

Rhoda McVey from Inverness had owned her two black and white cats, Struie and Meallie, for four years when she decided to move them north to live with her elderly parents. Her mother had gone into hospital, where she was to spend the last years of her life, and Rhoda would take Struie in to see her there. He always managed to cheer her up by providing purrs and cuddles, luxuriating on the elderly lady's bed and giving her lots of attention.

After Rhoda's mother passed away the two cats both spent a lot of time with her dad, who was now living alone. He had never expected to outlive his wife, and hated being on his own. They would accompany him whenever he did his gardening, and curl up beside him whenever he took an afternoon nap. They were his best friends for the last three and a half years of his life and made a huge difference to him. Speaking of that difficult time, Rhoda said: 'My cats mean the world to me. They made my parents' final years so wonderful.'

In recognition of their supporting roles, Struie and Meallie were honoured with The Special Award at the Rescue Cat Awards 2008, organised by Cats Protection, and also listed as finalists in the Best Friends category that year.

JOEY

When Carol Markt of West Linn, Oregon, adopted Joey from a shelter, she knew straight away he had a successful future as a therapy cat ahead of him…

Carol Markt's cat Joey had an important job – he was a feline therapist at Oregon Health Sciences University (OHSU) in Portland, Oregon. When Carol first adopted him from a shelter she could tell that he would be perfect for the job. 'He's incredibly relaxed and people-oriented,' Carol explained.

A typical day at work would see Joey being towed around the corridors of a hospital in an open cart. People he passed would pet him, and he seemed to enjoy letting them scratch his chin. Then he would spend a portion of his day with individual patients, curling up alongside them and purring loudly.

For example, he helped a 10-year-old boy named Stuart to recuperate after a kidney transplant. The cat sat with the little boy as part of the patient's rehabilitation process. 'He's really cool. He makes me smile,' Stuart commented, giving the cat a big cuddle.

But Carol's most special memory of Joey in action is the time when she brought him to sit with a teenage girl who had undergone brain surgery and wasn't responding to anything. Carol asked the girl's mother if she liked cats. 'I sat down by the girl with Joey on my lap and put her hand on him. Soon, she scratched him. Her mother was absolutely thrilled.' Joey's comforting presence had prompted the girl's first reaction since her surgery.

Joey and Carol's other cat, Nick, were part of the Pet Assisted Therapy Program that was founded in 1992 by OHSU Volunteer Services. Therapy cats in the scheme provide patients of all ages up and down the USA with confidence-building affection and comfort. The directors of the programme also believe that the cats help improve patients' mobility, memory, communication, pain management and self-esteem. All participating animals are screened and certified through the Dove Lewis Emergency Animal Hospital's Animal Assisted Therapy and Education Program and have to meet strict regulations on cleanliness, health, temperament and obedience before they are approved for the scheme.

Pets as therapy

In the UK, the charity Pets As Therapy (PAT) trains up animals including cats as therapy animals, and takes them to visit patients in hospitals and care homes around the country. Registered volunteers accompany the animals on their visits, which aim to comfort and provide companionship to people of all ages. There are around 4,500 PAT dogs and 108 PAT cats in the UK, visiting over 30,000 people every single week.

Amanda Crosthwaite from Hereford had never owned a cat, until a confident ginger tom strode into her life and befriended her. The friendly feline, soon to be known as Feet to Amanda, has been making new friends ever since and has made some new ones for Amanda too, including one very special lady named Margaret…

“Feet arrived at my home in Belmont, Hereford, in 1998 when I was at my lowest. My marriage had failed and I was at a loss with life. Then one day this handsome young ginger prince wandered into my house like he belonged there

and I fell in love with him. I had not had a pet since I was a child. Growing up we could never have a cat due to my mother not liking them, so Feet really has taught me how to respect animals and appreciate caring for a pet. ”

Amanda was thrilled with her new friend, but it was a while before she discovered where he had come from.

“ *Feet was approximately nine months old when we first met and at first I thought he was a girl! He spent the next six months with me constantly – I assumed he was a stray and bought him a collar with my telephone number and named him Feet. He had big paws so at first I thought of naming him Paws, but then I thought no, why not call him Feet instead? It was a bit silly but really suited him. Everyone agrees it does.*

It was the following day I received a phone call from his owners to say that Feet was called Orlando and actually a male! He only lived six doors from me in our cul-de-sac. I was very apologetic and made friends with my new neighbours quickly and explained how he turned up on my door. The lady that originally owned him told me that he arrived on a huge frozen chicken truck at Sun Valley chicken factory where her husband worked as a security guard. He had freezing cold paws and was cared for by the security guards at Sun Valley. They fed him titbits from their sandwiches. Then one day one of the guards brought him home to his wife to live with their ten other cats, six doors from me. ”

Though Feet technically belonged to Amanda's neighbours, that didn't get in the way of her friendship with him. And over time, Amanda began to learn of some of Feet's other adventures.

“ *As the years passed Feet was still called Feet and continued to visit me every day and spent every evening with me at home.*

I soon discovered that Feet had a daily routine when I was at work that involved travelling around the Belmont part of Hereford in the local yellow hopper bus service. The elderly ladies at the bus stop would fuss over him, get on the bus and he would join them. The driver got to know him – once the bus got back to the first stop he would drop him off again.

Feet would also walk a quarter of a mile to the McDonald's drive-through and had been seen by many people eating titbits from customers who sat outside on the benches in the garden. He was recognised from miles around!

On one occasion I was looking outside my bedroom window and saw Feet sunning himself in the middle of the cul-de-sac. A car drove towards him and he remained on his back, legs up in the air, and the car had to slowly go up the curb to not run him over. As the wheels went past him he gently struck out with his paw as if he was playing with the wheels. It was so funny to see and I thought: wow, how brave is my cat?! ”

A few years on, Amanda was facing some changes in her life. How would her friend Feet fit in with her new plans?

“ *After five years living in Belmont I met someone and we wanted to share a house together. His was the bigger house so it made sense to move in with him. That left the dilemma: would I be able to keep Feet permanently and could he officially become my cat? I asked his owner and she agreed straight away that Feet should be with me as our bond was so strong. I was overjoyed and moved Feet to his new pad on the other side of Hereford.*

Feet soon settled in, strutting his stuff, marking his territory and making himself known to other tomcats and making friends with elderly neighbours. My hours grew longer at work and I saw less of Feet and started to wonder where he was spending his day. I soon discovered that he was visiting a recently widowed elderly lady called Margaret. Margaret lived opposite our house and we had never properly met. I introduced myself and from then on we became very close friends. I started to visit her a few evenings per week for a chat and to check that she was OK and if she needed any shopping. Feet would always pop over for the visit and our main topic of conversation was all about

Feet. Feet brought a lot of therapeutic calmness, support and joy into her life as she had spent over 25 years with her husband and when she lost him she did not have any children to visit her, only relatives. For three years myself and Margaret would not go more than a few days without talking and she became a mother to me, and that was all due to Feet bringing us together. ”

What Feet had started became a lasting and life-changing relationship for Amanda. When she decided to move from the area, Feet became the link that kept her friendship with Margaret strong.

“ *Three years ago my partner and I decided to move to the country and bought a cottage 20 miles from Margaret. It was very upsetting telling Margaret our news but we quickly came up with a plan that Feet would visit every Thursday, and this has continued to this day for the past three years. Every Thursday I pop Feet into his cat basket, strap the seat belt over him in the front seat and drive 20 miles to drop him off with Margaret for the day whilst I go to work. They have a wonderful day together and Margaret always plans the day around Feet and never leaves the house as she values every minute with him. When I collect him at 6 p.m. Feet is usually asleep on his blanket with a half-eaten bowl of prawns left on the kitchen floor.*

Myself and Margaret have a catch-up over a cup of tea and then Feet is driven back to the countryside.

At my new home Feet is very settled in with our chickens, geese, sheep and the new addition to our herd – a dog! Feet has made it clear to the dog, Jess, that he is top cat and Jess is always put in her place by him.

Both Feet and Jess go for walks together with me in the woods for miles. He sometimes does a certain meow sound that I know means "carry me", which I do. ”

Through the years and all the changes Amanda has gone through, Feet has remained a constant companion in her life.

“ *Feet has had such a massive impact on my life. I have no children and he is like a child to me. Not only this, but through Feet I met Margaret and gained a mother figure in my life too. He is loved and known by so many people and at 12 years of age he looks like a teenager. He sleeps above my head on my pillow every night and follows me around like a shadow.* ”

Feet certainly is a special cat and has even become somewhat of a celebrity. In 2002 Feet came runner-up in the Kite Kat Kattitude competition in *House Beautiful* magazine, which featured a story about his visits to McDonalds and his adventures on the local hopper bus. In 2008 he made a guest appearance on the *Midlands Today* news after his photo was entered into the 'Big Picture' – Amanda had to send in a story with the picture, in which she told of his weekly visits to see Margaret. This was filmed and shown on television, and some radio interviews with Amanda and Margaret talking about Feet followed. Later that year, Margaret suggested that Amanda enter him into the Cats Protection Rescue Cat Awards – Feet was short-listed as runner-up in the Best Friend category. Well, he truly has been a best friend to Amanda.

> “*Feet is amazing and so individual. I am privileged to have such a remarkable feline as Feet. I have never been able to believe how a cat can have such an impact on so many lives and never hold a conversation with anyone – only a meow!*”

UNLIKELY FRIENDS

The old belief that cats and dogs can't live in harmony is disproved once and for all in this section, in which you will read about one very touching relationship formed between a cat and a dog, and with a few other species besides. These cats all seem to share one thing in common – an innate compassion for other living creatures. In some cases it is clear that a cat's maternal instincts take over, say, when fostering a family of abandoned ducklings, but precisely what prompts a cat to strike up a long-lasting friendship with a bear or an orang-utan remains a mystery!

HIROKO

To most cats a pair of succulent looking ducklings would make for an irresistible snack; or so Norio Endo from Japan feared when he accidentally left his cat Hiroko alone with his newly hatched baby ducks…

Norio Endo had bought a pair of spot-billed duck eggs from a farmer in Sugito village, Japan, and brought them home to wait for them to hatch. Sure enough, after some time two beautiful ducklings emerged from their shells. But in an absentminded moment, Norio left to go out, closing the door to the room the ducklings were in behind him – and shutting his three-year-old cat, Hiroko, inside.

Later realising his mistake, Norio returned and opened the door fearing the worst... only to find a contented looking Hiroko snuggled down next to the two ducklings, as if she were their proud mother. Since that moment, Hiroko continued to care for the ducklings as her own. She would groom them carefully and keep them warm with her body heat.

Hiroko had lost a litter of three kittens shortly before adopting her new family, which would explain in part her strong maternal instinct towards the defenceless creatures. Nevertheless, it was still quite a surprise for Norio when he first discovered the trio together!

MUSCHI

Maeuschen the black bear lived a lonely existence in her solitary enclosure at Berlin Zoo. That was until a little black cat named Muschi turned up and befriended her...

Muschi is nothing special to look at – just a normal black cat. But she has played a special role in the life of Maeuschen, or 'little mouse', a black bear that she befriended at Berlin Zoo back in 2000.

None of the staff at the zoo know where the mystery cat came from – she seemed to appear out of nowhere and strike up an unlikely friendship straight away with the zoo's 40-year-old Asian bear, Maeuschen. Heiner Kloes, a member of the zoo's management board explained: 'She appeared from nowhere in 2000 and we decided to leave them together because they got on so well. They sunbathed together and shared meals of raw meat, dead mice, fruit and bread.' Muschi (meaning 'pussy' in German) soon had her own fan club amongst regular zoo visitors.

The strength of their bond was tested in October 2007 when Maeuschen was moved to a temporary cage while her enclosure was extended. Zoo staff soon found a very distraught-looking Muschi hanging around outside the bear's cage, obviously pining for her companion of seven years. The keepers decided to allow the cat into the cage so that the old pals could be reunited. 'They greeted each other and had a cuddle and now they're happy,' said Heiner Kloes.

Black cats – lucky or not?

In Britain a black cat is seen as a bringer of good luck and prosperity, but it hasn't always been that way. In medieval times, British people reviled black cats as witches' familiars or imps in disguise, and many suffered cruel torture or were put to death. In some areas of Europe and North America the black cat's history of being mistrusted has left its mark, and so it is white cats that are believed to be lucky. Other cultures have selected certain breeds of cat as lucky symbols: in Russia the Russian Blue is seen as lucky, and in Thailand cats of the grey Korat breed are often given to brides to bring them good fortune.

LIBBY

At the age of six, ginger tabby Libby voluntarily became a full-time carer and seeing-eye cat for her life-long best friend, a dog named Cashew…

Animal lover Terry Burns and his wife Deb live in Middleburg, Pennsylvania, with their four dogs and two cats, including ginger tabby Libby and Labrador-Shar Pei mix Cashew. Libby had grown up having Cashew around and when the elderly dog began to go deaf and lose her sight at the age of about twelve, Libby stepped into the role of guardian.

By the age of 14 Cashew was completely blind, and Libby stayed by her side constantly, leading the dog around obstacles and helping her find her food bowl at meal times. The pair would sleep together in a shed, where Libby would leap to her feet and place herself squarely in front of Cashew if Terry came in, as if to say: 'Leave her alone, she's sleeping now.' The only time the pair were ever separated was when Cashew was taken out for a walk.

Without Libby at her side, there is no doubt that Cashew would have felt lost and very lonely. Libby had never received any training or prompting – she just seemed to instinctively know what to do for her friend. When Cashew passed away Libby was visibly bereft, and missed her canine companion for a long time. Their deep friendship proved that animals of different species can understand and help each other. In 2008, Libby was named Cat of the Year by the ASPCA in recognition of her selfless and heroic acts of compassion.

TK

A stray ginger tabby brought the twinkle back into the eyes of a depressed orang-utan at Zoo World in Florida...

When 43-year-old Sumatran orang-utan Tondalayo lost her mate, she became very depressed and introverted. She was too old to be moved to another zoo or to take another mate, and so staff at Zoo World in Panama City Beach, Florida, were very concerned for her health.

Two years later, an employee introduced a stray ginger tabby that had wandered into the zoo to Tondalayo, and the pair hit it off from the word go. TK (short for 'Tondalayo's Kitty') and Tondalayo would play together, cuddle and sleep together at night.

Almost immediately, staff at the zoo noticed a huge improvement in the orang-utan. 'It's an unbelievable match,' said the zoo's education director, Stephanie Willard. 'This has worked out a lot better than I expected. She's got brighter eyes now. He's brought a lot of light to her.'

MANCAT

In Australia, a rescued cat named Mancat proved to be indispensable to the Jordans when he became a guide cat for their elderly pug dog…

When Adrian Jordan found a litter of six newborn kittens dumped in a rubbish bin near his work place in Australia, he felt he had no choice but to bring them home. He and his wife Anne took care of the little kittens and bottle-fed them. When the time came, five of the kittens, all female, were picked out by cat lovers who were more than happy to give them new homes. But no one seemed interested in taking the sixth kitten, a black and white tom, and so the Jordans decided to keep him and christened him 'Mancat'.

The Jordans had always kept pet dogs, and so Mancat grew up alongside them and was always at ease with his canine friends. One of them, an elderly black pug named Mary, he got on particularly well with, and the pair seemed to form a special bond.

Mary was blind in one eye due to an old injury, and as she got older the sight in her other eye began to fade. By the time she was 14 she had gone completely blind, but the Jordans only realised what had happened because of a change in Mancat's behaviour. Mary's loyal feline friend became very attentive to her; he would walk alongside Mary wherever she went, guiding her carefully around furniture and even accompanying her on toilet trips out to the garden. At meal times he was by her side, making sure the other dogs didn't pilfer Mary's dinner, and when it was time to go to sleep he guided her to bed.

Things got more difficult for Mary with age, and the Jordans did what they could to help; they built a set of little steps up to their bed so that she could climb up to her usual resting place, and every night faithful Mancat would be there to help the old dog make her way up the steps and would curl up alongside for company. Mancat kept up his duties for two years, until Mary passed away peacefully at the grand old age of sixteen.

CHIQUITA

A canny cat called Chiquita in Brazil struck up an unlikely friendship with a bird, but her motives didn't appear entirely noble…

Chiquita belonged to Nair de Souza, who lived in Porto Alegre, Brazil. One day Chiquita spotted a young injured bird that had fallen from its nest and went to investigate. So far, so feline, but what she did next was somewhat unexpected.

Rather than gobble up this sitting duck of a treat as most cats would, Chiquita instead adopted the little bird. The pair became so close that they would eat from the same plate. Mrs de Souza was amazed by her cat's behaviour, but welcomed her pet's new friend into her home all the same, christening the bird Pitico. 'Pitico has even started to eat meat, because the two of them only eat together,' she marvelled.

However, it would appear that Pitico was something special as far as Chiquita's attitude towards birds was concerned, as the cat had by no means seen the last of her bird-hunting days. In fact, the unsuspecting Pitico was to play a supporting role in the cat's sport: 'Chiquita uses Pitico to catch other birds. It is really unbelievable!' exclaimed the cat's stunned owner.

Nesting

Wendy Hobbs from Reepham, Norfolk, came across a cat up a tree in her garden that appeared to think it was a pigeon. At first she thought the tortoiseshell stray was stuck, but soon realised it had set up home in an abandoned bird's nest. It would leave the tree to beg for food at her back door then return to its eyrie. 'I don't know why she loves the tree,' said Mrs Hobbs. 'She sits there watching the traffic. My husband and I think the nest must have been a pigeon's because it's so messy.'

MISTY

A farm cat named Misty came to the rescue when a litter of baby skunks were rejected by their mother at a private animal farm in Three Hills, Alberta…

Misty was a farm cat that had recently given birth to and successfully weaned her own litter of kittens. So when a mother skunk rejected her young a week after they were born at the GuZoo centre in Three Hills, Alberta, staff knew Misty would be the perfect candidate to take over maternal duties.

Misty certainly didn't turn her nose up at the task – soon after she was photographed feeding the baby skunks as if they were her own kittens. The caring cat fed the litter for two weeks, and remained with them even after they had been weaned onto solid foods.

MAX

When Hayley Thomas from Sleaford, Lincolnshire, brought home a stray kitten, her pet tomcat Max was more than happy to lend a helping paw in getting the newcomer settled in…

Hayley Thomas from Sleaford, Lincolnshire, worked in a veterinary clinic as a nurse. One day a newborn stray that had been attacked by another animal and sustained terrible injuries was brought in. Though Hayley already had a pet cat, a ginger tom called Max, she decided to adopt the poor stray and nurse her back to health at home.

Milly, as Hayley named the kitten, didn't just have Hayley to rely on – Max immediately stepped up to the task of helping her get back on her feet. For the next six weeks Hayley nursed Milly, and Max was always nearby to help. He would keep the kitten company, groom her and feed her. If she was distressed he would rush over to comfort her, and when she grew stronger he played with her and even gave her a crash course in how to use a litter tray!

Hayley was thrilled to see Milly blossom into a confident and loving cat, which she put down in part to the affectionate Max, for teaching Milly everything a cat needs to know. Hayley described her number one cat as placid and sweet-natured – a typical ginger tom that loved to laze around and was always up for a cuddle, whether with another cat or with his mummy.

MEDICAL WONDERS

It is extraordinary the lengths and expense some cat owners will go to in order to ensure their cat's well-being. Even more astonishing is what some cats can endure, and still have a good quality of life. The stories in this section are testament to cats' resilience, and the strength of the bond that can form between cat owners and their pets. Recent developments in technology and science have meant that many health problems in cats that would have previously resulted in them being put down can now be resolved or at least alleviated. Cats may even play an important role in medical research, as one unique cat in this section shows.

DRAGGIN' BEAR

A grey kitten in Ashland, Oregon, suffered a broken back in a vicious attack by a raccoon and was left a paraplegic. But thanks to the groundbreaking work of a veterinary surgeon at the Bear Creek Animal Clinic he was given a new lease of life and a unique way of getting around…

When a concerned student brought a stray kitten that had been attacked by a racoon into the Bear Creek Animal Clinic in Ashland, Oregon, Dr Alice Davis could see straight away that the poor animal's back was broken. His back legs were paralysed and Alice knew that he wouldn't be able to walk on his own again, but something about the grey cat made her fall for him and want to give him a chance.

Alice nursed the kitten back to health, and began to think about how she could improve his quality of life. After doing some research on the Internet, she and her fiancé Gordon Sievers came up with a plan. They would construct a wheeled frame that would support the cat's back legs and allow him to drag himself around using his two functioning front limbs. After experimenting with a few different versions, the pair successfully created a chariot made out of K'NEX, the popular construction set product. This versatile toy is usually used by children (and adults) to create cars, rollercoasters or whatever their imagination desires. They added a sling made from a headband to support his body, and Velcro ties to keep him in place.

Strapped into his four-wheeled cart, Draggin' Bear – as he was named, in reference to the clinic and his method of getting about – was soon entertaining staff at the clinic by tearing around at top speed. 'He doesn't seem to know or realise he's different,' said Alice. 'He's one of the most playful kittens I've ever seen.' Though he would remain paraplegic for the rest of his life, as it wasn't possible to correct the injury through surgery, Alice felt confident that Draggin' Bear would live a long and fulfilling life. She planned to build bigger chariots for him as he grew larger.

Looking after Draggin' Bear comes with extra responsibility – Alice has to help him go to the toilet and keep him in a cat-nappy as he isn't able to control his bowels fully. 'We take him everywhere,' she explained. 'You can't just let anyone pet-sit him.'

Draggin' Bear became a lucky mascot for the Bear Clinic – he even has his own website, www.dragginbear.com, where there's a friendly invite to visitors to the Ashland area to 'stop by and pay him a visit'. The cat's heart-warming story of enjoying life against all odds has been made into a book, *Little Draggin' Bear: The Cat on Wheels* by Leia Tait.

ERNEST

A partially blind black and white cat named Ernest from the Isle of Wight wears contact lenses to help him see…

Contact lenses are not the easiest things to apply, so you can imagine that trying to put them on a cat would be nearly impossible. But that's exactly what happened to Ernest, a 15-year-old black and white cat; and he wouldn't be able to see without them.

Ernest arrived at the RSPCA rescue centre in Godshill, Isle of Wight, after being injured in a car accident and has lived there ever since. The cat suffers from entropion, a condition in which the eyelids roll inwards, which causes inflammation and impairs vision. Centre manager Paula Sadler first noticed something was wrong with Ernest when he kept squinting at things and had trouble seeing where he was going.

Because of Ernest's age, the operation to treat the disease could have been life-threatening, but luckily a creative vet came up with an alternative solution: he fitted the cat with contact lenses. Ernest's new lenses set off quite a transformation, as Paula explained: 'Now his eyes have opened up and he has a new lease of life. The lenses have worked wonders.'

KIKI

Virginia Sanders opted for an unconventional treatment for her Siamese cat Kiki's asthma…

Kiki, an 11-year-old Siamese cat belonging to Virginia Sanders, had suffered with asthma and a bad cough for three years. She had been treated with cortisone injections, but Virginia, an alternative therapist from South Africa, was concerned about the effect that the injections would have on her cat's liver in the long term.

She decided to approach a holistic veterinarian to see what alternative treatments could be offered, and he recommended that she try a rather unconventional treatment for cats: acupuncture, a system of complementary medicine in which fine needles are inserted in the skin at specific points along supposed lines of energy.

Virginia sat in with Kiki during her acupuncture treatments to soothe her. After three sessions, Virginia noticed a vast improvement in her cat's asthma, though she still had the usual health problems that older cats suffer from, such as a stiff back.

Vet Dr Barry Hindmarch explained that alternative treatments such as acupuncture can be used on animals to relieve the symptoms of a range of conditions, including kidney problems, skin problems, chronic arthritis and even the feline form of AIDS. Homeopathic methods have been used to treat infertile horses and cows with udder infections.

When an animal is treated holistically, first there is an examination of its medical history, natural diet and surroundings. The aim is to find a natural treatment option. As Hindmarch explains, animals have emotional problems – they grieve, get anxious and traumatised, and holistic treatment extends to this part of their well-being, treating them as a whole rather than just their physical problems.

'All conventional treatment methods are exhausted before we decide on a holistic method,' said Hindmarch. 'With alternative medication we try to improve the animal's quality of living.' In Kiki's case, it certainly seemed to have worked.

Alternative therapy for cats

In recent years there has been an increase in awareness of alternative and complementary medicine, with many people seeking out these treatments for themselves. It is not surprising, then, that some people want these options to be available to their pets. It has taken some time for the veterinary profession to accept complementary therapies in the treatment of animals, but the Royal College of Veterinary Surgeons has now stated in its Guide to Professional Conduct that they recognise the importance of vets informing their clients about all the treatment options available. There are now several organisations and websites that provide information about these therapies for animals, including the Alternative Veterinary Medicine Centre. Acupuncture and chiropractic treatments are the most frequently applied to animals, but other treatments include physiotherapy, aromatherapy and massage, traditional Chinese medicine, homeopathy and herbal medicine.

BABY

Accident-prone Baby was lucky enough to survive two falls from the third floor of a building, and earned the name of 'bionic cat' after successful operations left her with implants in every limb…

Baby, a white cat with brown and black markings, might just be the world's only bionic cat. She fell from the window of her owner's third floor apartment in London when she was just a kitten. Fortunately, veterinary surgeons were able to help her walk again by putting metal pins into her front legs, which were badly broken.

At the age of six, Baby was brought into the Blue Cross Animal Hospital in Victoria, London, after another fall from her owner's window. Her back legs were both broken and she needed extensive surgery and further implants in her back legs. 'Baby is extremely lucky to be alive,' commented Jess Gower, Blue Cross chief veterinary surgeon at the hospital, who carried out the operations after Baby's second fall.

Jess Gower explained that, 'Contrary to popular belief, cats don't always land on their feet – Baby landed on her back.' Baby was put onto a frame after the operations, but Jess hoped that after eight weeks she'd be able to walk normally again, thanks to the implants. 'We were stunned to find it was the second time she had done it,' said Jess, who wasn't aware of the cat's previous fall until she took an X-ray. 'Now she has metal implants in all four legs, staff decided to call her the "bionic cat".' From the outside, you wouldn't be able to tell that there was anything unusual about Baby, as she can walk completely normally.

The Blue Cross provides treatment and care for the pets of owners who cannot afford private vets' fees, and covered the cost for Baby's extensive operations. Of course, not all cats are fortunate enough to receive such expert treatment. Veterinary staff at the hospital warned Baby's owner of the danger of leaving the window of her high-rise flat open. 'She's had two lucky escapes but needs to be very careful to keep her remaining lives intact,' said Jess.

CADBURY

Most cat owners will agree that there's nothing more welcoming than coming home to be greeted by a meowing and purring cat. When Jean Kelly's cat Cadbury lost his voice because of a dangerous rare condition, she was prepared to do whatever it took to help him recover and get it back...

Jean Kelly, a public relations manager who lives in Olney, Buckinghamshire, was very attached to her beloved pet cat, Cadbury. She had got him when he was just five months old. He had followed her sister home one night, but as her sister was too busy to care for a cat, Jean had agreed to look after him for a week. Cadbury was not in a good state – he was very skinny and had a huge white flea collar around his neck which was practically choking him. But for Jean it was love at first sight, and she realised at the end of the week that she'd have to keep the gentle, friendly cat. 'He loves sitting in the sun in the conservatory, and waits outside for the schoolchildren when they walk home in the afternoon,' she said. 'I once counted eight hands all stroking him at one point. He just loves it.'

When Cadbury suddenly lost his voice at the age of thirteen, Jean was understandably distressed. The cat began breathing with his mouth open and making a strange noise like a wind-tunnel, so she immediately took him to the vet to find out what was wrong. The vet didn't have good news for Jean – when he examined Cadbury he discovered the cat was suffering from a paralysed larynx, and would need immediate surgery to save him from this very rare and dangerous condition. 'I was told that Cadbury needed an emergency operation or he would die,' explained Jean. 'They were concerned because he also had a heart murmur, but they finally agreed to operate.'

To prevent the paralysed larynx from blocking Cadbury's throat and allow him to breathe again, he had to undergo two operations to tie back his swollen voice box. After the operations he was in an oxygen tent for six days, then moved to intensive care for several days more. It took four months for him to recover, during which he was nursed at the vet's surgery and had to cope with the added complication of an underlying thyroid condition. The whole process, including after-care and check-ups, left Jean with a whopping bill of £10,000 – and it saved Cadbury's life.

Jean remarked, 'It was never about me – it was about Cadbury and his quality of life. I know he's not a young cat but I wanted to give him a fighting chance.' She had been planning a dream holiday – a safari in Namibia – but had to cancel it and scale down her plans to a caravan holiday when the vet's bill came in. Her insurance company, PetPlan, paid out £6,000, but she had to find the remaining £4,000 herself. 'But the money was worth it just to see Cadbury well again and happy,' said Jean, who was just glad to have Cadbury back home again, enjoying his favourite dish of tuna and meowing contentedly.

Love beyond the grave

Cat lovers are well known for their dedication to their feline friends, and it's understandable that any loving owner should want to provide for their beloved pet after their own life has ended. But some cat owners have taken this to extremes:

- In the eighteenth century, the Earl of Chesterfield and the Second Duke of Montagu both left their pet cats considerable pensions in their wills.
- A Mrs Walker from England left £3 million to an animal charity, provided the organisation care for her cat for the rest of his life.
- Ben Rea left £7 million to be split between three charities and his own pet cat.

MR GREEN GENES

Mr Green Genes is the world's first glow-in-the-dark cat, and has played an important part in research into cures for diseases such as cystic fibrosis…

Sixth-month-old Mr Green Genes is a normal ginger tom, but when the lights go out his eyes, nostrils, gums and tongue glow green under ultraviolet light.

Scientists in New Orleans working on research into cystic fibrosis modified the cat's DNA to see whether a gene could be introduced harmlessly into an animal's genetic sequence. They picked a gene that glowed under ultraviolet light so that they could track where it went in the cat's body – green fluorescence protein, the gene in question, tends to express itself in mucous membranes, so that's why Mr Green Genes' features light up at night.

Betsy Dresser at the Audubon Centre for Research of Endangered Species in New Orleans gave her assurances that the added gene would have no effect on Mr Green Genes' health. 'Cats are ideal for this project because their genetic make-up is similar to that of humans,' she explained.

The scientists hoped that use of the fluorescence gene would make cystic fibrosis easier for them to spot. In the long run, the aim is to create a 'knockout gene' to combat the cystic fibrosis gene and other diseases.

ULTIMATE SURVIVORS

Cats have often been said to have nine lives, and the stories in this section would certainly have you believe that to be true. Another saying goes that curiosity killed the cat, which could easily have been the case for many of these characters – from cats plunging from high-rise buildings to one particular feline suffering a spin through a combine harvester, there is adventure and suspense worthy of any action film to be found here. Their ability to survive and recover from the most horrific accidents and life-threatening situations is truly awe-inspiring.

TABITHA

Jessie Sculpher from Barmston, Yorkshire, had only had Tabitha, a rescue cat from Cats Protection, for three days when the tabby went missing. Tabitha, eight years old at the time, went through a terrible ordeal before the two were reunited again…

“*I brought Tabitha home from the rescue centre in Reighton on a Monday. They told me to keep her inside for the first few days. By the Wednesday she seemed to be settling in quite well. But when I got up on Thursday she was nowhere to be found. I looked everywhere and a friend came round to help me look but there was no sign of her – we couldn't understand it.*”

Jessie put up 'missing cat' signs around the village, hoping to hear news of her new pet. Weeks went by and nobody responded. Then one night something woke Jessie from her sleep…

“*It was exactly 44 days since Tabitha had gone missing when I woke up at 4 a.m. and heard a thumping noise. At first I thought I might have left the back door open so I went to check, but it was shut and locked. I live in a bungalow and*

I'm always very careful about locking the door. Then as I passed the bathroom I heard another thud and a faint meowing. Hearing all this on my own in the house at four in the morning – well, you can imagine what I was thinking. ”

Jessie went into the bathroom, where the noises seemed to be coming from the cupboard unit under the washbasin.

“ *The back of the cupboard is hardboard and stands about five or six inches away from the outer wall, leaving a gap for the water pipes. I could see four legs sticking out at the bottom of the hardboard. I got down on my hands and knees and broke the hardboard away – my arms were cut and bleeding. I pulled Tabitha out by her legs and put her onto the bathroom floor. She couldn't stand or anything, she was just rolling around and was very weak.* ”

After a traumatic night, Jessie phoned the vet the next morning. It was Saturday so they were running an emergency only service.

“ *The vet, Duncan, wasn't there when I called, but the girl who answered the phone knows me so she got hold of him on his mobile. He drove from Driffield three miles away to come and see to Tabitha. When I explained what had happened he said to me, "Didn't you hear anything before? She had been there for forty-four days.* ”

Duncan examined Tabitha and explained to Jessie that she was severely dehydrated and put the cat on a drip. But what was more worrying was the brain damage the animal had suffered – she had been in a coma for 44 days. That would explain why Jessie never heard a sound during all that time. Jessie realised that Tabitha must have squeezed through the narrow gap at the top of the hardboard backing in the cupboard, then hit her head as she fell down the gap between the cupboard and the wall.

“ *Tabitha was on a drip and receiving treatment for three and a half days at the vet's. When I got her home she only weighed eight pounds. I had to gradually increase her food as she slowly got better. Now she weighs about a stone!* ”

Tabitha made a full recovery, the only noticeable difference being a slightly droopy eyelid, as you might see in a person who has suffered a stroke. Jessie keeps her indoors as she can't bear the thought of anything happening to her outside after all she's been through.

“ *She's a healthy and happy cat who enjoys watching people through the window. My neighbour often sees her there and pops over to say hello. The vet was lovely with her when she was ill and always asks after her when I take her in for her flu jabs. He says to me, "I don't think you should call that cat Tabitha – I think her name should be Miracle."* ”

Tabitha was honoured with a Rescue Cat Award from Cats Protection in 2008, as winner of the Most Incredible Story category.

UNSINKABLE SAM

Oscar was a seafaring black cat that spent time on ships in both the German Kriegsmarine and the British Royal Navy during World War Two. His seeming ability to cheat death earned him the moniker of 'Unsinkable Sam'...

Oscar began his seafaring career onboard the German battleship *Bismarck* during World War Two. When the *Bismarck* set sail on its first mission on 18 May 1941, Oscar was aboard. And when the ship was sunk following a dramatic battle on 27 May of the same year, he was amongst a small number of survivors: only 115 of the ship's 2,200-strong crew were not lost at sea. Oscar had the good fortune to be rescued by sailors on board the homeward-bound British destroyer HMS *Cossack*, when crew spotted him floating on a plank, just hours after the battle had subsided. So it was that the black cat changed sides and became the *Cossack*'s mascot: it was the crew of this ship that gave him his name.

Oscar held his position of ship's mascot on HMS *Cossack* for some months, during which time the vessel was involved in convoy escort duties in the Mediterranean and North Atlantic. On one such voyage on 24 October 1941, the *Cossack* was sailing from Gibraltar to the United Kingdom when it came under fire from the German submarine *U-563*. The ship received severe torpedo damage and 139 crew members were killed in an explosion that decimated one third of the front section of the ship – the rest of the crew, including Oscar, were moved to HMS *Legion*. Attempts were made to tow the badly damaged *Cossack* back to shore, but eventually it had to be abandoned to the deep. Oscar had survived another shipwreck, and after this second scrape with death, sailors back at the base in Gibraltar gave him the nickname 'Unsinkable Sam'.

In a strange twist of fate, Oscar's next posting was aboard the aircraft carrier HMS *Ark Royal*, a vessel that had played an important role in the sinking of the *Bismarck*. On 14 November 1941, as the ship made its way back from Malta, the *Ark Royal* was hit by a torpedo fired by German submarine *U-81*. The mission to tow the damaged vessel back to Gibraltar failed once again as water seeped in, causing it to roll over and sink just 30 miles from the base. Oscar, true to form, was found clinging on for dear life on a bit of floating wood. Thankfully on this occasion, because the ship sank so slowly, all but one of the crew were saved. It was Unsinkable Sam's final military sea voyage.

Oscar was transferred back to the base at Gibraltar, where he spent some time working as mouse-catcher in the naval offices, and then to the United Kingdom. The only known feline to have survived three shipwrecks in the space of a year, the tenacious cat lived out the rest of his days on dry land, in the safety of a Sailor's Home in Belfast. He is said to have lived until 1955, and a pastel portrait of Unsinkable Sam (*Oscar, the Bismarck's Cat*) by Georgina Shaw-Baker hangs in the National Maritime Museum, Greenwich.

LUCKY

A grey-and-black-striped moggy called Lucky lived up to his name when he survived a somewhat unorthodox exit from his owner's high-rise apartment in Manhattan…

Keri Hostetler was cleaning her flat in lower Manhattan one day and had opened the window of her home office to get some air circulating. A short while later she was looking around the flat for her three-year-old cat Lucky, when she saw that the door to the office was ajar and the window flung wide open. And through the window she could see some window cleaners who were working on the building across the street gesticulating wildly at her.

These workers weren't just waving to pass the time – they were trying to tell Keri that they'd just seen her cat step out of her office window and plummet 26 stories to a balcony on the sixth floor below. One of the workers, John Hayes, had even managed to get three shots of the extraordinary fall on his camera, showing Lucky as he stepped out into thin air, mid-fall, and the landing. He was able to direct Keri to where he'd seen Lucky land, and there she found him curled up on the cover of a barbeque grill.

Keri rushed her cat straight to the vet's but was relieved to discover that the only injuries he'd incurred were a broken toe and lower jaw. One thing she knew for sure – she'd picked the right name when she'd decided to call him Lucky.

Free-falling felines

Statistics show that 90 per cent of cats recorded to have fallen from multi-storey apartment buildings have survived the fall. In Ypres, Belgium, cats' fabled ability to land on their feet used to be tested in a somewhat cruel annual tradition where cats were dropped from the tower of Cloth Hall. During the Middle Ages cats were brought in to control rodent populations, and the annual 'cat throwing' took place once that year's stocks of cloth had been sold and the cats were no longer needed. Most of them ran away unharmed.

The tradition is still maintained, but thankfully only soft cat-shaped toys are now used in the ceremony – the last time live cats were used was in 1817.

So how do cats make a safe landing? It's all to do with the way they rotate their bodies in mid-air, ensuring that they land feet first. A cat held upside down and then dropped from only 30 cm above the ground can right itself in less than two seconds in order to land on its four paws. The forequarters flip round first, swiftly followed by the head and the hindquarters. It then spreads its limbs ready for landing, which also helps to slow its descent and reduce impact with the ground.

JOEY

John and Sharron Scrupps from Middleton, Leeds, would often foster young kittens, looking after them until a permanent home could be found for them. But one little white and tabby kitten that came to stay stole their hearts, and proved to be one in a million…

“*Joey came to us as a four-week-old foster kitten and had been found wandering on a very busy road by a member of the public. His eyes were huge and very badly damaged – in fact, he*

resembled more of an alien than a kitten! We knew he needed his eyes removing as it was obvious that they were very painful and he couldn't see out of them. They would swell and swell until they ruptured and he would utter the smallest cry as it happened then settle down until he went through it all again the next day.

Finding a vet to do the operation was to prove very difficult. Everyone was saying that Joey would be better off being put to sleep as he was in pain and would have no quality of life, but we saw something in this little alien kitten that seemingly no one else could. We saw character, a massive sense of fun and a determination to overcome things. ”

While the Scrupps searched for a vet to perform the operation, Joey was already fearlessly finding his way around.

“ *If Joey head-butted an obstacle he would try again, each time moving slightly further along it until he had worked out its dimensions, then he would continue until he found the next obstacle. Later on he would learn to use his whiskers and other senses, but for now he was happy to use his own head-butting technique.* ”

Eventually the Scrupps finally found a vet willing to operate on Joey – he was seven weeks old when he had his surgery.

> *When we went to collect him from the vet's later that day we were expecting a drowsy little kitten; however, what we were met with was a reception desk full of people shrieking and laughing. When we finally got to the front it was to see this tiny white and tabby kitten trying to catch the fingers of the staff as they typed on the keyboard and the best laugh was the amazing accuracy that he had in catching them. At last Joey was completely pain free and ready to take on the world and all it had to offer.*

John and Sharron regularly foster kittens, rearing them until they are old enough to move to a new home. But this time, it was different.

> *Because Joey was a foster kitten we were supposed to raise him to ten weeks old then put him up for adoption, but having been with him through all these difficulties we felt we couldn't let him go. In short, we had fallen head over heels in love with him. So Joey was officially adopted into the Scrupps household where he was going to, and still does, give endless love and entertainment and have a very good quality of life.*

And so Joey, with his new lease of life, settled in to the Scrupps' household, soon becoming an indispensable part of the family.

> *For a couple of years Joey led a normal life. He went out into the garden with our other cats, he climbed on top of the shed and wandered around the cul-de-sac visiting neighbours, and we took him into our local primary school regularly to teach young children about disabilities in animals. We wanted to teach them that euthanasia is not the answer to blindness for an animal. All it takes is patience, time, education and of course oodles of love, and a blind cat can have a very good quality of life. It's important that the children see Joey is not actually very different from any other cat.*
>
> *Joey became known locally as the sleepy-eyed cat because he looks just like he has his eyes closed and unless it is pointed out most people don't even notice he has no eyes. He loves to explore the classroom areas in schools and loves the attention of all the children.*

As he grew older, Joey also began to play an important role in caring for the foster kittens that the Scrupps would take in.

> *Joey worked for us and the agency we fostered for by "mothering" the little foster kittens we take in. He would play with them and teach them how to stalk and pounce and lots of other little skills a young kitten would normally learn from its parents. He would shepherd them all into a chair and curl round them whilst they slept to keep them safe and warm.*

But then in the summer of 2007, when he was three years old, Joey's idyllic life was to take a very frightening turn.

"Joey had taken to his favourite spot in the middle of the garden and was relaxing in the sun when a stray dog managed to get through our fencing and spotted him. The dog flew at Joey and before we could do anything Joey had panicked and run the length of the garden and jumped the fence, which would take him out into unfamiliar territory. Even more worrying, the dog was still in pursuit. We jumped into the car and drove round and round the estate calling out for Joey and friends and neighbours scoured the streets and sheds or anywhere that Joey may have hidden for protection. All that night we searched, calling out for Joey, rattling his biscuits in his dish, anything that might encourage him to come out if he were hiding and afraid. We did the same the following day and on and on for two weeks. We rang all the vets in the area; we put up posters. We drove and walked round the estate; we knocked on doors and asked people to check their outbuildings. We did everything we could think of, including asking our local parish priest to pray for Joey's safe return.

After two weeks we felt that time had almost run out for Joey. We didn't know if the dog had caught him and he was injured somewhere or if he had been hit by a car. Joey had never had to fend for himself like this before. How was a blind cat going to cope on his own? How would he catch his food? How would he survive other attacks in unfamiliar places? Would he know where to find some shelter from the wind and all the rain we were having at the moment? We were frantic. Of course we hoped that someone had picked him up and taken him in, but there were posters everywhere so they would surely know we were looking for him and we were offering a reward for his safe return. ”

Three more weeks passed and with it the Scrupps' hope passed too – they had begun to mourn Joey's loss.

“ *We put away Joey's dishes and washed and folded his special blanket into a cupboard out of sight, it was just too painful to see these things and not know what had happened to him. The kittens we had in were missing him too. They wandered round looking for him and found it difficult to settle in the chair without him. We had to roll a large towel into a giant sausage and put it on the chair with them but it wasn't the same. Everyone missed Joey.* ”

Another week passed by, before Sharron received a phone call out of the blue.

“ *As we were sitting down to tea the phone rang. "Are you Mrs Scrupps?" asked an unfamiliar male voice, "cos I think we have found your cat." My heart stopped and I struggled to find the words, "Is he alive?" "Oh yes love, he just invited himself in for tea!" I couldn't speak. The voice then said "He may be a bit hurt, though, because he won't open his eyes." That was all I needed; I just sobbed down the phone: "He hasn't got any eyes!" Then, in between laughter, tears and near hysteria we managed to get the address and within fifteen minutes we were there.* ❞

The Scrupps were thrilled to be reunited with their beloved pet, and equally astonished by what he had been through.

❝ *Never have I experienced such emotion! It turned out that Joey had run in one direction and gone through a huge housing estate and had been living on some wasteland near the motorway. He was very thin, very dirty and had fleas and ticks galore but he was our Joey and he was back from the dead! The following day after Joey had been bathed, combed and debugged he was settled on the coffee table on his special blanket and looking like nothing had ever happened. The kind people who had found him refused any reward except a card and bunch of flowers from Joey.* ❞

John and Sharron had no idea how Joey had survived all this on his own – they could only guess that he used his amazing hearing to capture small animals to eat. Once he was settled back in, they were keen to make sure he couldn't be separated from them again.

Joey now has a safe outdoor area which we built for him, but he still likes to go visit our neighbours from time to time and his school visits have now resumed along with his kitten-fostering duties. ”

In 2008 the Scrupps nominated Joey for a Rescue Cat Award, and he was shortlisted by Cats Protection as a finalist in the Ultimate Survivor category.

“ *Joey is what you might call an ultimate survivor, but I guess he really has had to be!* ”

In 2007, the town of Methley, near Leeds, was badly affected by the terrible floods that summer which damaged thousands of people's homes and businesses. Julia Malloch discovered that every cloud truly does have a silver lining when the floods brought lovable cat Noah into her life…

Julia Malloch and her daughter were out walking near their home in Methley, Leeds, when they saw three cats clinging onto a floating branch. It was being carried along on the flood water that had swamped the field in which he and his two brothers were living during the floods of summer

2007. There followed a dramatic rescue, in which some teenaged boys constructed a makeshift raft and made their way across the water to the frightened cats and brought them safely back to dry land.

Julia and her daughter, who had witnessed the whole rescue, couldn't resist taking one of the traumatised and soaking moggies, a black and white cat, home with them, and christened him Noah. Once they got him home they dried him off and helped him recover from his terrible ordeal. He was so adorable that they fell in love with him straight away and adopted him as their pet.

The floods had brought misery to thousands across the country, but to Julia and her family they had brought Noah, and they were able to transform his life and give him a lovely home. In return, he became the most wonderful family pet for which they could have hoped.

A mischievous tabby named Mindy managed to baffle a whole station full of policemen in Peterborough, and used her head to get herself out of a pickle…

A motorist who saw a tabby cat wandering near the A47 in Peterborough was understandably concerned when he realised she had a jam jar stuck on her head. But when he approached the cat he was even more astounded to discover what had enticed the cat to put her head in the jar in the first place – a live field mouse! The jar was wedged firmly around the cat's neck with the terrified mouse just inches from its jaws – a race against time was on to free the clearly uncomfortable cat and rescue the mouse from almost certain death.

Unable to dislodge the jar himself, the worried driver took Mindy, as was later discovered to be the cat's name, down to Thorpe Wood Police Station to see if anyone there could help. The receptionist tried to ease off the jar with no success and so summoned three burly police officers. But whichever way they twisted it and however hard they all pulled, the jar just wouldn't budge.

A spokesman for Cambridgeshire police described the spectacle: 'It was like a scene from *Tom and Jerry*. No one had seen anything like it. We were worried the cat was going to suffocate or that she would be badly cut if we broke the glass.' The police called on the help of the RSPCA, but before they could arrive on the scene, Mindy took matters into her own paws. Casually strolling across the room, she went up to a wall and knocked the jar against it, smashing it with one blow. Luckily for the mouse, it managed to escape before Mindy had time to pounce.

After the dramatic incident was over the police took Mindy to be checked out by a vet. She was completely unscathed and was microchipped, so they were able to reunite her with her owner in Peterborough just two miles from where she was found. And what about poor Jerry? 'As for the mouse, as far as we know it's still running around the police station.'

FELIX

Mandy Parsall from Brentwood, Essex, lived in a house that backed onto some farmland, so she thought that her pet cats would be quite safe there, away from the dangers of a busy road. But Felix still managed to get himself into quite a scrape…

Mandy Parsall got two kittens, Felix and Jasper, in 2002 from her local Brentwood and Basildon Cats Protection rescue centre. They were part of a litter of four kittens; two male and two female. As Mandy had recently lost a pair of elderly male cats, she was keen to give a new home to the two tomcats. Felix was named after the cat in the Felix cat food advert because his markings were so similar, and Jasper was named after the comedian Jasper Carrott because the kitten was always up to mischief. The pair of cats settled into their new home, and all was well until one evening in the summer of 2005.

" *One summer evening we heard that a cat had become entangled in the combine harvester cutting the fields behind our house and been badly injured. As Felix wasn't at home at the time, we immediately started searching for him everywhere. All the neighbours helped, looking in garages and up and down the streets. The search went on for twenty-four hours and we had started to fear that Felix was dead. At about five in the evening, my next door neighbour called to say that Felix was dragging himself through her garden. I went outside to see him pulling himself through our hedge, before collapsing on the patio. I was so shocked – that he was alive, and at the terrible state he was in – that for a while I was rooted to the spot. It was only when my neighbour shouted to me to phone the vet that I sprang into action. I called our vet, Nitzan Kroter, who asked if Felix was the injured cat that had been reported the day before – when I said yes, he told me to wrap him in a towel and bring him in to the surgery in Brentwood. My partner Frank rushed me and Felix there in the car. After checking that none of his internal organs were damaged, the vet made the decision to remove Felix's injured tail and right back leg – they were amputated the next day. All went well with his recovery and Felix eventually returned home.* ”

Mandy was relieved that Felix had survived the ordeal and was able to come home so she could look after him in the comfort of familiar surroundings. But Felix wasn't out of the woods just yet.

> *Unfortunately, after a few days he became very unwell and was rushed back to the vet, who was puzzled as he said Felix was displaying all the symptoms of tetanus (previously unheard of in cats). Tests confirmed tetanus, so the race was on to save Felix. The antidote was obtained from the local equine centre and the vet calculated a dose for a cat. Felix, now paralysed and choking, was hospitalised again at the vet's and treated for tetanus.*

Tetanus is a medical condition characterised by prolonged contraction of the skeletal muscle fibres. As the infection develops it causes muscle spasms in the jaw, often referred to as 'lockjaw', and elsewhere in the body, and also stiffness and rigidity of certain muscles. The disease has long been known in humans, and it is often found in horses – but up until this point it was unheard of in cats. So at the time there was no way of knowing for sure whether the treatment would be successful and, if it was, whether Felix would make a full recovery. It was a groundbreaking case in veterinary science, and Nitzan Kroter, the vet who treated Felix, later published a paper on feline tetanus in a journal. Mandy was at Felix's side through it all, giving him lots of love and care, hoping that he would get better and be allowed to come home.

> *I visited him daily and massaged his poor body and three legs. After a couple of weeks his front paws began to move and he tried desperately to stand, but unfortunately his remaining back*

leg was still paralysed. Treatment continued and then one day he managed to stand and totter forward. Everyone at the vet's was so excited and eventually Felix returned home. ”

Back at home, Felix settled back into his routine, and after a week he was keen to get out and about again and back to normal. Mandy was happy to see that he hadn't lost any of his character or joie de vivre.

“ *This brave cat now tears around on three legs and is still the most loving and best friend in the world.* ”

In 2008 Mandy nominated Felix for a Cats Protection Rescue Cat Award, and he was singled out as the winner of the Ultimate Survivor category. Felix has also received attention from journalists and television programmes, and the amazing story of his accident and recovery was featured in an episode of an eight-part series made by Maverick Productions and aired on BBC Three in autumn 2009 called *Bizarre Animals ER*.

Bizarre ER

The television programme that featured Felix's story, *Bizarre Animals ER*, covered a range of 'the oddest animal accidents and strangest pet problems from all corners of the UK – from domestic pets and farmyard animals injured in unusual circumstances to weird emergencies experienced by wildlife'.

Some of the felines that made an appearance on the show were a cat that survived a 60-degree spin in a tumble dryer, a tomcat that had a sex change and a cat that spent a 30-mile, 60-mph journey trapped inside an engine compartment.

SASSY

Sassy was the only animal left unaccounted for after a veterinary clinic collapsed during a tornado in Windsor, Colorado. She was trapped under rubble for two hours before being rescued…

A tornado that tore through Windsor, Colorado, hit the south-eastern part of the city particularly hard. One of the worst affected buildings was the Garden Valley Veterinary Hospital, where Jane and Richard Matt of Windsor had left their 14-year-old cat Sassy in the hospital's boarding facility while they drove to their grandchild's graduation ceremony in Arizona.

After the tornado hit, the couple's daughter, Laura Pascavis, called them to tell them the news. Their immediate concern was for their granddaughter, who was dog-sitting for them at their Windsor home. Laura reassured them that their dog and granddaughter were quite safe, but had to tell them the bad news that the veterinary hospital where their cat Sassy was boarding had been destroyed in the storm. She had seen a news report that showed the extent of the damage – the walls had collapsed and the roof was gone.

Jane and Richard were now very anxious for Sassy's safety. They had had the cat for 14 years and were terrified at the thought of losing her. That evening, their daughter Laura was watching the news when she saw incredible footage of Sassy, who had been rescued from the rubble by the owners of clinic, Dr Rick Dumm and his wife Martie. The pair had been helped by several others as they dug through the debris in search of the missing cat. They worked for two hours in a rescue effort in which Rick used his truck to shift mounds of rubble before they found her. All the other animals had been safely removed from the facility after the storm, but then staff realised that Sassy was missing. They were relieved when they heard her calling to them from the rubble and were determined to get her out alive.

Laura quickly phoned her parents to tell them that Sassy was alive and well, and the couple sent an email to the news channel, expressing their gratitude to the clinic staff for rescuing their pet and saying how relieved they were that she had been found unharmed. The reporter on the news channel said that Sassy's rescue was the only bit of good news he'd had to report that day.

Luckily, the couple's Windsor home had not been badly damaged – many other homes in the area had been seriously affected. The Garden Valley Veterinary Hospital built a temporary facility to house and care for animals while their building was restored, and received plenty of offers of support and help during this difficult time.

PRECIOUS

A Persian cat named Precious was alone in her owners' apartment opposite the World Trade Center in New York when the 9/11 terror attacks happened. The building was badly damaged and declared unfit for use, so the Kerrs thought they had seen the last of their beloved pet…

Shortly after the attacks on the World Trade Center of 11 September, a missing pet cat was discovered on the roof of her owners' damaged apartment block on Liberty Street opposite the World Trade Center.

D. J. Kerr and her husband Steve had gone away when the attacks happened, and had organised a house-sitter to call in at 10 a.m. on 11 September to check on Precious, a house cat that had never been outside before. But she never made it round there – when the Twin Towers collapsed the windows in the apartment were blown out and it was filled with glass, metal, dust and smoke, and the whole building was declared unsafe for occupancy for at least nine months.

The couple assumed that their cat hadn't made it and tried to come to terms with their loss. But then, on 2 October 2001, rescuers were called to the building because people could hear a cat crying. With the help of a recovery dog they located the injured and terrified animal on the rooftop and managed to capture her. Precious had eye injuries and had suffered from smoke and dust inhalation. She also had burns on her paws from the heat of the building following the explosions.

The rescue workers brought Precious to the Suffolk County SPCA van that was parked nearby, which was being used to treat rescue and search dogs for exhaustion and exposure. Suffolk SPCA chief Roy Gross thought that she had probably only managed to survive for so long without food by drinking from the puddles of dirty rainwater on the roof.

Precious' owner said: 'It's unbelievable. It's a miracle. I can't believe she's alive.' The cat needed a course of treatment for her eyes, but the vet expected her to make a good recovery. 'I gave her her favourite food – sliced turkey,' said Kerr, who was overjoyed to be reunited with her pet. 'She was eating so fast because she was starved to death and she's drinking a lot of water, but she's so happy, she's just purring.'

CASPER

In 2006, the Frankish family from Seaford, East Sussex, lost five of their six cats in a horrible house fire that destroyed their home. But one little survivor, a grey long-haired cat named Casper, gave the family hope…

Helen Frankish from Seaford, East Sussex, already had four pet cats at home, but couldn't resist two beautiful semi long-haired cats that she came across at a rescue centre.

“*We homed Casper after finding him in a rescue centre with his companion, Molly. He was five years old at the time. We were struck by how handsome Casper was immediately we saw him; ghostly smoky grey, semi long-haired, with gorgeous bright golden amber eyes. Molly was a lovely contrast, another semi long-haired cat, jet black with bright green eyes – they made a striking pair. The rescue centre explained that both had been very badly treated and Casper in particular was very nervous and frightened and it took a long time for us to win his trust – for weeks we couldn't go anywhere near him, but we persevered and eventually won him over. We already had four other cats and he and*

Molly settled in to our cat family. It was lovely to see Casper slowly find his feet and make friends with our existing pets; he was jumpy and nervous but he gained confidence over the weeks and months and it was very satisfying to see him settle. ”

Things were going well in the Frankish household – little did they know that difficult times were just around the corner.

“ *Unfortunately, however, six months later we had a terrible house fire. The firemen were confident that the cause was an electrical fault from a kitchen appliance. Ben [my son] and I had only left the house 45 minutes earlier when we got the emergency call from our neighbour. We were very lucky the fire wasn't earlier or at night when we would have been asleep, as although we had smoke detectors, the fire took hold so quickly we would soon have been trapped upstairs. As a result of the fire we had to be re-homed while our house was renovated. We lost a lot of personal effects but the devastation was made much worse because five of our beloved six cats died. Thankfully, Casper survived – mainly due to the hard work of the fireman who endeavoured to resuscitate him for 20 minutes, and we are so grateful.* ”

Casper had miraculously survived the fire – but he wasn't out of the woods yet.

> *Casper was at the vets for a week for treatment, he was seriously ill for some time and we were very frightened we would lose him, but the vets said he would perk up every day when we visited, and seeing Casper helped us to focus on being positive when things seemed very bleak. After a couple of weeks, Casper was well enough to leave the vets so he came to stay with us in the hotel where we were housed temporarily, and then in a rented house for several months before we could return home.*

It was a time of great upheaval for the Frankish family, and yet Casper seemed to be coping extraordinarily well.

> *Despite the fact he had obviously been so badly treated by a previous owner and had been an extremely nervous and frightened cat, Casper coped exceptionally well with all the trauma, the treatment, and the disturbance and stress from moving into different accommodation several times – he amazed us at how well he adapted.*

Eventually, Helen and her family were able to return home and get back to normality, despite all that had happened.

> *Some six months after the fire we returned home and have subsequently homed several kittens to establish a new cat family, and Casper has*

taken them under his wing as their foster dad and they all live very happily.

Our friends who met Casper when we first brought him home say he is unrecognisable from the terrified cat they first met – he could not cope if anyone went in the same room as him, let alone try to touch him. Now, he comes for strokes and tickles, and even plays with and grooms his "foster family" when they need "licking in to shape"!

'The only lasting effect of the fire has been a rather nasty cough that affects Casper from time to time. Thankfully, he doesn't have it very often now, but it is a sobering reminder of the fire, and how very lucky we are that Casper managed to survive. ❞

In 2008, in recognition of everything that Casper had been through, Helen nominated him for a Cats Protection Rescue Cat Award and he was listed as a finalist in the Ultimate Survivor category.

❝ *Considering Casper was so badly treated that he flinched if you went near him when we first got him, it has been wonderful to witness how his confidence has grown and what a loving and kind-natured cat he is despite everything he's been through. We were worried that the effect of the fire would traumatise him and mean all the trust and friendship we had built with him would be lost, but he has survived against the odds and the fact that he survived kept us going when we were going through a terrible experience. Nothing will take away the immense sadness at the loss of our other furry friends, but the fact that Casper has obviously grown to love and trust us, despite his bad experiences, and that he has been able to settle in to a happy life, being a positive role model to his adoptive "family" and enjoying the companionship of other cats has been very rewarding.* ”

Debbie Duke was distraught when she discovered that her pet cat Lucy had disappeared from her home in Kent, even more so because she was just about to move 600 miles away to Scotland…

Debbie Duke, her husband and two children were all packed up and ready to move from their home in Meopham, Kent, to a new house in Inverness, Scotland. They had finished packing all the furniture and left Lucy, the family pet, behind in the house while they spent the night in a hotel nearby. They planned to collect her the next morning before catching their flight to Scotland.

But when the Dukes arrived at the house in a taxi to collect Lucy, she was nowhere to be found. They searched everywhere and even enlisted the help of their neighbours in the search, all to no avail. With the meter on the taxi running and the time until their flight ticking down, they were forced to make the difficult decision to leave without Lucy. They hoped that their friends and neighbours would find Lucy and put her on the next flight up to join them. 'Every one of us was heartbroken,' said Debbie, 'I wept all the way to Scotland.'

But Lucy didn't show up later that day, or for a long time after that. The Dukes' old neighbours had promised to keep searching for her, and so they put up 'missing cat' posters all around the neighbourhood, notified the police and local vets and posted her photo on a missing pets website. After weeks of no news, the Duke family began to give up hope of ever seeing their cat again.

Seven weeks after she had last seen Lucy, Debbie Duke received a phone call from the new owner of their old house in Kent. After he had moved in he had begun to hear strange noises in the house. On closer inspection they appeared to be coming from under the kitchen floor, and on listening carefully he realised they were pitiful meows. They were coming from Lucy, trapped beneath the floorboards all this time.

The new occupants rescued Lucy from confinement and she was taken by the RSPCA to Meopham Veterinary Surgery. Heidi Cooper, the vet who examined her, thought she was dead at first. 'I have never seen a cat look so frail and still be alive,' she said. The 14-year-old cat had gone seven weeks without access to food or water and was in a critical state; it is thought she survived by licking water condensation from the piping under the floor.

The Dukes were both relieved to hear that Lucy was alive and horrified to hear of the ordeal she had been through. They realised that a panel board under one of the kitchen units may have been removed to accommodate the washing machine, leaving a space just big enough for Lucy to squeeze through.

Lucy had lost almost a kilogram, which is a lot for a cat, and was severely dehydrated. She was given specialist treatment, and the Dukes were relieved to hear that she was back eating solid food again within five days. After weeks of convalescence at the home of friends of the Dukes, Brian and Marion Glover, she was deemed fit enough to make the journey to her new home.

Mr Duke travelled down to collect the family's beloved pet. The flight and the veterinary treatment had come to about £1,000, but Mr Duke said it was worth every penny to get her back. Reunited with her lovely cat Lucy once more, Debbie said, 'We never believed we would see her alive again. It broke our hearts to leave Kent without her. To have her back is a real miracle.'

EMMY

A cat called Emmy survived a nightmare ordeal when she was accidentally locked in a shed in her owner's garden in Torquay, Devon…

Black and white Emmy must have walked unnoticed after her owner into the garden shed at their home in Torquay, Devon. Without realising, her owner locked the door when he had finished what he was doing inside, leaving Emmy trapped. Emmy's owners spent weeks looking for their missing cat, only to discover her emaciated form inside the shed nine whole weeks after they had last seen her.

A spokesperson for the RSPCA said that the 10-year-old cat had managed to survive by licking condensation from the windows of the shed, which were covered in lick marks. She was taken to the Blue Cross Animal Adoption Centre in Watcombe, Devon, and at first the staff didn't think she would make it – she was so weak and skeletal.

Emmy's owners decided to give up their pet as they were so distressed at the trauma they had put her through accidentally. They had also moved house and weren't sure that their new home would be suitable for the cat.

Emmy was shaken by her ordeal, but made a full recovery. Staff at the centre in Watcombe described her as a hardy cat with a determination to survive. Understandably, she had a fear of tight spaces and of being left alone, but staff were confident that she would still make a loving pet for the right family, and were all set to find her a new home. 'If only she could speak and let us know how she got through it because she has an amazing story to tell,' said Laura Valentine, who cared for Emmy during her time at the centre in Watcombe.

LACY

When Keira-Jane Keegan's kitten Lacy was snatched by a sea eagle from her garden in Sydney, she didn't expect to see the little cat again…

Keira-Jane Keegan was playing with her ten-week-old kitten, Lacy, in the garden of her home in Sydney, Australia. Suddenly a sea eagle swooped down into the garden, grabbed the kitten by its head and flew off. It happened so fast that Keira could do nothing but watch as her little pet was carried off in the bird's talons. Even had she reacted in time, it is unlikely that she could do much to stop such a powerful bird.

But then, in a strange twist to an already dramatic story, the eagle dropped Lacy about a kilometre away in another garden. The owners of the house discovered the kitten in their back garden and took her to the local RSPCA centre.

She had nasty head wounds, which needed stitches, and she was put on a course of antibiotics to make sure she didn't develop any infections.

Meanwhile, Keira hadn't given up hope on her pet and had been making calls to animal shelters in the hope that the kitten had survived and been handed in. Eventually the pair were reunited again. The vets who treated her said it was a miracle that she survived being dropped from such a height.

Sea eagles are the second-largest bird of prey found in Australia and feed mainly off sea creatures such as fish, turtles and sea snakes. But this eagle obviously fancied something different for dinner!

Voodoo fall

In Queensland's Gold Coast in Australia, a seven-year-old Manx cat named Voodoo disappeared from his home on the thirty-fourth floor of a high-rise building and was discovered a day later under the broken branches of a bush directly below the window that must have cushioned his fall. Owners Sheree and Wayne Washington said the cat had always had an affinity for heights – they would often see him teetering on the edge of their balcony. Voodoo walked away with nothing more than a bloodshot eye, a scratched ear, a cut mouth and a damaged paw.

INCREDIBLE JOURNEYS

Some cats seem to have an uncanny ability for finding their way back home – even when they have been transported miles away into unfamiliar territory. Yet more astonishing is when cats are separated from their owners and manage to relocate them in a completely new location. Some researchers believe that cats have magnetised cells in their brains which act as an internal compass, helping them to sense direction, but this hasn't been proved – the homing skills of cats remains somewhat of a mystery.

Other cats have been unwittingly or consentingly taken along with people on epic journeys across the globe, and this section includes a few 'firsts' for felines – the first cat to circumnavigate Australia, and the first cat to cross the Atlantic, for example. Then there are the adventurous cats that just can't seem to stop going off exploring, whether that's on foot or by the lazier option of taking the local bus.

MIA

Mia's incredible story began when she became trapped in a lorry at Suzuki's site in Ezstergom, Hungary. In a journey that took over a week, the pregnant stray travelled all the way to Milton Keynes, where she was to begin a new life…

Francesca Robinson, from Northampton, worked at Suzuki's Milton Keynes site. One day, some rather unexpected goods showed up at the warehouse.

“*That day was a normal morning. I went to the ice rink and lapped up the feeling of freedom that my skates gave me as they moved quickly across the ice, the exhilaration of a jump and the frustration of my spins. I walked into work that day with the same old grin, threw my skates onto the desk, changed and answered the phone. It was security. I smiled as they told me that one of my packages in the delivery from Hungary was making a noise! They were security and it was the company's package – surely they could open it, I thought to myself. Anyway, I walked down to the warehouse and there in a box were two of the tiniest kittens you have ever seen. One black, his eyes closed to the world, and a little tabby with a white*

> *neck trying to lie over him protectively. Not since my rescue dog Meg had found her way into my arms at the age of 12 had I felt this way. I had never had a cat in my life, but there was an instant bond between us. I watched some of the hardest men in the warehouse find a high-vis jacket to keep the kittens warm, and one got them water.* ”

It seemed that the kittens had been born on a lorry that had arrived at the warehouse that morning. But where was their mother?

> “ *By this time the cats' story was circulating. A lorry had arrived from our Hungarian factory and as it was being unloaded by forklift a cat had jumped off – a tabby. They had chased her but she had run out the door and into the undergrowth. This turned out to be the kittens' mum. Or as I know her now, my beautiful Mia.* ”

Mia must have somehow got trapped in the lorry before it left Suzuki's site in Ezstergom, Hungary. The lorry had been on the road for a week since then, so it was a miracle that she had survived – especially as she was heavily pregnant. Vets thought that Mia had survived by licking condensation off the sides of the lorry. Francesca began making arrangements for the kittens to be moved from the site – but it wasn't as straightforward as she first thought.

> “ *A charity was phoned to collect them; if only they had said at the start that they didn't collect*

international strays. It was the end of the day when after repeated calls to the charity the staff were told to call the local Trading Standards, who arranged a collection of the kittens. Two ladies arrived in a van. I ran downstairs and asked where the kittens were being taken. I was told that it was unlikely they would survive the night. I tried to hold it together as I demanded to know where they were going. One lady turned to me and whispered "Four in Hand". I didn't know what she meant. They left promising to bring a trap the next day to try to catch the other cat. ”

Francesca now felt very involved in the little kittens' fate; she wanted to find out exactly where they were and make sure that they would be safe.

“ *Well, thank goodness for the Internet – typing in "Four In Hand" revealed a quarantine centre in the next county. I phoned the centre straight away and spoke to a lady who was very unfriendly. The kittens hadn't arrived at that point and I got a lecture on the cost and how the kittens without their mother didn't stand a chance. I told her I was prepared to pay their way, but she had heard it all before and was quite dismissive. I promised to phone the next day about the kittens. That night thinking the kittens would be destroyed I felt I had let them down, and let tears stream down my face. The next day I phoned the centre; the kittens had survived the night, despite being very weak. I asked about visiting them. I was told coldly to come at the weekend.* ”

Francesca was determined to find the kittens' mother and reunite the little family, and kept a close eye on the trap that had been set up in the warehouse in the hope of capturing the missing tabby.

“ *It was a bank holiday weekend and I spent it driving over to work to check the trap for the mother cat. Over that weekend we trapped rabbits, hedgehogs and every small mammal imaginable and I embarrassed myself at my local Tesco – they were distributing free packs of cat food, which happened to be perfect for bating the trap. With a processed meat factory across the road the chance of catching the mother felt slim. On the Tuesday morning things felt bleak, but a phone call to the office came. Security told me there was a cat in the trap! And they had stopped one of the lorry drivers from releasing the cat. It felt like slow motion walking across the yard with a couple of concerned colleagues. As I reached the trap my eyes met a frightened young cat, and something clicked between us that has never been undone. I made an unspoken promise to give her a safe home for life – her amazing strength had touched my heart.* ”

Francesca had at last managed to capture Mia, and felt certain already that she would give a home to the stray cat. But she couldn't take her home quite yet.

The same ladies collected Mia. As she was on her way to the centre I ran upstairs and phoned the centre and told them that the mother was coming in. Later, I was told that Mia had accepted her kittens immediately and cleaned them before collapsing with exhaustion. ”

The three cats would have to go through quarantine before they would be allowed to stay in the UK. As Francesca had pledged to pay the cats' way, she was to be left with an impressive vets' bill.

“ *Their six months in quarantine had begun. I started to put money where my mouth was and I began to see Kay, the cold lady who answered the phone, thaw. I returned religiously every Saturday to visit the kittens, a 70-mile round trip that I looked forward to each week. I soon realised that Kay's frostiness was because so many people promise to assist animals but when they realise the scale of the cost they shy away and disappear. This wasn't an option for me, even though the only way for me to pay was to take equity out of the house and accept monetary gifts from family and friends. Soon I understood Kay's outlook as people who stood up and said they would take one of the kittens faded away as they realised a significant amount of money was involved. In a way I was relieved; I had fallen in love with my little family and wouldn't have separated them for anything. I remember my mother telling me that if I had to choose I should take the mother, as the kittens would find homes more easily. I nodded in agreement, knowing in my heart that they were all coming home with me.* ”

After a long wait, the three cats were declared in the clear and allowed to leave the centre.

“ *The six months passed and before I knew it I had three little faces ready to come home. They piled into the car with so much affection from all their carers at the centre. These were the people who had shown them genuine love throughout their short lives. I smiled as they travelled home without a murmur. I realised that they were born travellers.* ”

There had been brief family discussions about the kittens being adopted, but as time passed and the kittens settled in to their new home, that began to look increasingly unlikely.

“ *My mother sat with the three of them one morning and turned to me and agreed that they should never be separated. I couldn't help grinning and saying that decision had been made a long time ago.* ”

Some time later, Francesca nominated brave Mia for a Cats Protection Rescue Cat Award. She was singled out as a finalist in the Most Incredible Story category. Francesca had given Mia and the kittens the chance for a happy and healthy life together. In return, she received their unwavering and lifelong friendship.

> “*Almost three years to the day we sit here together. They have been by my side, Mia is my rock, the kittens – Ilya and Eva, both named after Olympic figure skating champions – play constantly. Mia adores her kittens. Since they came home we have rescued two bunnies and two guinea pigs. We are now a family of eight and everyone is equal. Only Mia thinks she needs to mother all of us, she is a very special cat and one who reminds me what life is all about. One lady who contributed to the cats' quarantine bill named her daughter Hope; well, these three have embodied that with all their worth.*”

KIDDO

In 1910, American explorer Walter Wellman and his crew set off in the *America* in an attempt to be the first to cross the Atlantic by airship. Little did they know, a feline passenger had stowed away on board…

Walter Wellman (1858–1934) was an American explorer, aeronaut and journalist. On 15 October 1910, Wellman and his crew of five men left Atlantic City, New Jersey, on the airship *America* to cross the Atlantic Ocean. If they succeeded, they would be the first to make the crossing by airship. What Wellman didn't know was that he had a sixth crew member aboard – a crew member's cat named Kiddo that had stowed away in one of the lifeboats.

The grey tabby didn't take well to flying at first– in fact, he made such a fuss meowing and yowling in protest that first engineer Melvin Vaniman sent an exasperated in-flight radio message (apparently the first in history) back to base that read: 'Roy, come and get this goddamn cat!'

Following this rather frosty reception, Kiddo was then shoved into a canvas bag so that he could be lowered into a motorboat beneath the airship and taken back to land. However, weather conditions proved to be too rough and so the crew were forced to accept that the cat would remain aboard for the voyage.

But once Kiddo had acclimatised to life in flight and found his balance, the crew were pleasantly surprised to discover that he was a useful crew member. Navigator Murray Simon noted that the cat was 'more useful than any barometer' and advised that no one should attempt to cross the Atlantic in an airship without a cat. Kiddo had an uncanny sense for predicting bad weather ahead. And if he was sitting out in his favourite spot on one of the lifeboat's sails, soaking up the sun, the crew knew they could relax for a while.

The airship *America* stayed in the air for 71 and a half hours, breaking the record for the longest continuous flight. She was 475 miles from reaching her destination when the engines failed and the crew were forced to bring her down near Bermuda. Kiddo and the crew were rescued by the steamboat *Trent*.

Back in New York the crew received a hero's welcome, and Kiddo became something of a celebrity – he was displayed for a time in leading department store Gimbel's, reclining on soft cushions in a gilded cage as people came to pay homage to the amazing airfaring cat. Kiddo spent a quiet retirement living with Walter Wellman's daughter.

A first for felines

In July 1919, a tabby kitten named Whoopsie outshone Kiddo by becoming the first cat to make the Atlantic crossing from Britain to America. She was brought aboard the British airship *R-34* by her owner William Ballantyne, who stowed away with her in a tight corner between the girders and the gas-bags. It wasn't long before Ballantyne became nauseous from the smell of gas and had to reveal himself. By then the ship was too far into its voyage to drop off the pair of stowaways, so, once recovered, Ballantyne worked his passage as cook and general factotum, and Whoopsie was taken into the care of George Graham, who at the age of 42 was the most senior airman on board.

The little cat proved his worth as a member of the crew by entertaining and comforting the airmen during the flight.

After 108 solid hours of flying, the airship came in to land at Long Island, New York, and was much celebrated for being the first to make the crossing. It spent just three days there before making the return voyage. Whoopsie became the airship's mascot until it crashed in 1921, from which he escaped with nothing more than a bruised paw.

TRIM

Trim was the first, and may still be the only, cat to circumnavigate Australia. He belonged to Matthew Flinders, an explorer who has been remembered in history for exploring and mapping much of Australia's coastline in the early nineteenth century…

Trim was a seafaring cat from the very start of his life, which began in 1797 aboard HMS *Reliance* on a voyage from the Cape of Good Hope to Botany Bay. The kitten fell overboard, but swam back to the ship and scaled a rope to get back aboard. This display of strong survival instinct and intelligence made him a favourite with explorer Matthew Flinders and the ship's crew. Flinders named the cat Trim after the butler in Laurence Sterne's *Tristram Shandy*, because he considered him to be a faithful and affectionate friend. The little cat was black, with white markings on his paws, chin and chest.

Trim accompanied Flinders on HMS *Investigator* as the explorer circumnavigated the Australian mainland, mapping much of the continent's coastline for the first time. He was also at Flinders' side when he set sail back to England aboard the *Porpoise*. The ship was wrecked on Wreck Reef (around 450 km east-north-east of Gladstone, Queensland) in 1803, but the pair survived. Flinders and Trim continued their voyage back to England aboard the *Cumberland*, but when the vessel was forced to dock for repairs in Mauritius, Flinders was accused by the French of spying and imprisoned. Trim shared his captivity until his unexplained disappearance, and Flinders wrote in his journal the following tribute to the faithful moggy:

> 'To the memory of Trim, the best and most illustrious of his race, the most affectionate of friends, faithful of servants, and best of creatures. He made the tour of the globe, and a voyage to Australia, which he circumnavigated, and he was ever the delight and pleasure of his fellow voyagers.'

In 1996 a bronze statue of Trim by sculptor John Cornwell was erected on a window ledge of the Mitchell Library in Sydney, right next to a statue of his owner, and the library's cafe was named after the cat. Trim also features on a statue of Matthew Flinders in Donington, England, the birthplace of Flinders.

GULLIVER

A Scottish cat stowed away in a toasty spot on board a coach, where he spent a 300-mile journey from Glasgow to Hull…

Mechanic Daniel Parnel was stunned to discover a young ginger tomcat in the engine of a National Holidays coach at the company's Hull depot when he removed a panel to clean the radiator. The furry creature was perched on the radiator itself, and at first sight Daniel thought it was rat, or maybe a squirrel.

The little cat had been on quite a journey – the coach had just come in from Arrochar near Glasgow in Scotland some 300 miles away. Daniel thought that the cat had probably crept on board in search of warmth, and gone to sleep in a cosy spot on the radiator.

Daniel christened the cat Gulliver, after the famous fictional world traveller. After getting him checked out by a vet he decided to keep the well-travelled feline. 'He hasn't done badly getting to Hull,' Daniel commented. 'It gets really hot in there.' Gulliver was thought to be one of the large population of feral cats that inhabits Arrochar.

SERGEANT PODGE

A 12-year-old Norwegian Forest Cat from Bournemouth baffled his owner when he began a mysterious night-time routine…

Liz Bullard had had Norwegian Forest Cat, Sergeant Podge, for 12 years when he suddenly took up a bizarre routine. It all began when the black cat went missing one day from her home in Talbot Woods, Bournemouth. Worried, Liz called the RSPCA and began phoning her neighbours, asking if any of them had seen him. Later that day she was relieved when an elderly lady who lived about a mile and a half away called her back to say that she had found the missing pet.

Liz collected Sergeant Podge from the lady's house, but within days he had disappeared once again. She rang the old lady and sure enough, Sergeant Podge was sitting outside her house once again. Every morning since then it became routine for Liz to drop her son off at school, then pick up Sergeant Podge from his collection point on the pavement outside the same house between eight o'clock and quarter past. Liz has never found out for certain why he makes this nightly trip, but she thinks he might be on the lookout for treats as a woman who used to live nearby had a habit of feeding him sardines.

The cat is thought to walk a route that takes him across Meyrick Park Golf Course. When Liz pulls up in her car, all she has to do is open the door and the cat, mostly to be found waiting patiently on the pavement, hops in for the ride home. 'If it's raining he may be in the bush but he comes running if I clap my hands,' Liz explained.

Annoyingly, Sergeant Podge hasn't cottoned on to the concept of school holidays and weekends – he makes his trip every day, so there's no chance of a lie-in for Liz. The main thing for Liz, though, is knowing that Sergeant Podge is safe and sound. 'I know where to collect him – as long as he's not wandering the streets.'

The long-haired cat became somewhat of a celebrity after tales of his nightly exploits were reported in the national press, and now he has is own website and profile page on Facebook where fans and admirers can log in to post messages to him and share photos of their own cats.

Norwegian Forest Cats

This is a breed that is perfectly adapted for the great outdoors. They have two coats – a thick, woolly undercoat to keep them warm and a waterproof overcoat to keep them dry. The name of the breed suggests wild origins, but in fact it has been a domesticated breed for many centuries. Norwegian Forest Cats enjoy human company and make great pets, but they love the freedom of exploring the outside world.

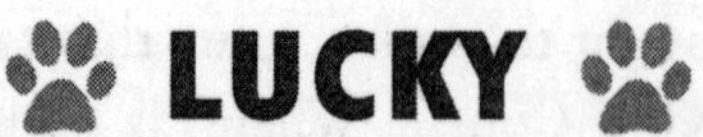

LUCKY

When Audrey and Alan Plumpton from Amersham, Buckinghamshire, went on their annual holiday to Brittany in France, the last thing they expected was to return with a furry new addition to their household…

Audrey and Alan Plumpton loved cats, and lived together with their pet cat, Sorrel, in Amersham, Buckinghamshire. Every year the couple would leave Sorrel in the care of a family member and go away on holiday together to Brittany.

“*For 26 years we have spent our holidays in a cottage on a beautiful golf course in France. There have always been feral cats which have mostly been black. This time, in September 2007, we saw two lovely little kittens with unusual colouring like Siamese cats playing around the wheels of our car. Before we leave the cottage to come home we always check the boot while putting our cases in to make sure none of the cats have got inside.*”

But on this occasion, unbeknownst to the Plumptons, a stowaway had crept aboard for the 280-mile journey home.

> “*We left the cottage at about 2 p.m. to travel to St Malo on the motorway and arrived there at about 4.30 p.m. We booked in to a hotel on the main coastal road and parked our car there overnight. We left the hotel at 9 a.m. the following morning to catch the 10.30 ferry to Portsmouth, arriving there at 6.30 p.m. We then had a car journey of over two hours to our home in Amersham where we were greeted by our granddaughter, who had been looking after our 19-year-old cat, Sorrel.*”

So far, everything had run to plan. But then the couple made an extraordinary discovery.

> “*Just as we were entering the house we heard this little noise coming from the bonnet of our car. When we opened it there was this tiny little kitten with bright blue eyes looking up at us. We thought he was trapped and rang the RSPCA, who couldn't come until the next morning, so we put some food inside the bonnet. He did come out occasionally and ran into our hedge but we couldn't catch him for two days until they brought a cage and eventually did so.*”

Audrey and Alan were only too happy to offer the kitten a home with them, especially after all he'd been through. But the well-travelled feline wasn't in the clear yet – all cats entering the UK from abroad are subject to a six-month quarantine period if they do not hold a pet passport.

> *We did our best not to have him put into quarantine as he was only six weeks old and had only been with his mother in an area where there has been no rabies. Our MP and DEFRA were contacted but to no avail. We visited him every week while he was in quarantine where he was so well looked after by the kennel maids at the quarantine kennels at Heathrow; they picked him up and cuddled him all the time.*

Eventually, the kitten was given the all clear and allowed to come home with them. It didn't take them long to think up a name for their new friend.

> *We thought Lucky was an appropriate name due to his circumstances. He really is the most adorable, intelligent and affectionate cat and we are so thrilled to have given him a happy life and that he has enriched ours.*

In 2008, the Plumptons nominated Lucky for a Rescue Cat Award in the Most Incredible Story category and he was chosen as a finalist by Cats Protection out of hundreds of entries.

CASPER

Bus drivers in Devon were amused to discover they had an unusual regular passenger – a long-haired cat called Casper…

Casper the cat belongs to Susan Finden, a care worker in her fifties from Plymouth. She adopted him from a rescue home in 2002, and had always thought he was quite an independent cat. In fact, she named him after Casper the Friendly Ghost, because he was always disappearing off on his own.

On one occasion he went off on an adventure to a car park a mile and a half away from Susan's home, and she had to carry him all the way back in a basket. But even Susan was surprised at her headstrong feline when she discovered he had become a regular passenger on the local First bus service and a familiar face to all the bus drivers on his favoured route.

Casper had got into the habit of catching the number three service from his home in Plymouth. Bus drivers had become so accustomed to him that they knew where to stop to let him off. None of them could be certain of what he would do when he got there, but he would always turn up to catch the bus again later to go home.

As he seemed to be a well-behaved passenger, the bus drivers didn't mind him hopping aboard without a ticket;

he would queue patiently with the other passengers, then calmly trot aboard and curl up on his favourite seat. A notice was even put up by the drivers in their staffroom, reminding each other to look after the furry passenger should they see him boarding their bus. Susan commented of her unusual cat: 'He does love people, and I don't know what the attraction is but he loves big vehicles like lorries and buses.'

Sadly, Casper was killed in a hit and run accident when crossing the road to board the bus one morning in 2010. Susan was devastated at the loss, and he will be sorely missed by the passengers and bus drivers to whom he had become a familiar and friendly face.

MRS CHIPPY

Mrs Chippy was a tabby cat that belonged to Harry McNeish, ship's carpenter aboard the *Endurance* during Shackleton's ill-fated voyage to cross Antarctica via the South Pole in 1914...

In 1914, Sir Ernest Shackleton set off with a crew of 28 men aboard his ship the *Endurance* in an attempt to make the first land crossing of the Antarctic continent. The conquest of the South Pole had already been made by Roald

Amundsen in 1911, but for Shackleton, a crossing of the continent from sea to sea remained 'one great main object of Antarctic journeyings'. The Imperial Trans-Antarctic Expedition is considered the last major expedition of the Heroic Age of Antarctic Exploration, and though it failed to accomplish this objective, it became recognised as an epic of endurance.

Mrs Chippy was the only cat aboard that ship and belonged to ship's carpenter Harry 'Chippy' McNeish. The cat's name was somewhat misleading, for Mrs Chippy was actually a tomcat. He became the ship's mascot, and took great delight in teasing the sledging dogs by leaping across the roofs of their kennels, tantalisingly out of reach. At the time, he would most likely have been the only feline to have travelled so far south on a sea voyage.

Sadly, Mrs Chippy and the ship's crew never made it across the Antarctic. The *Endurance* was crushed in ice in the Weddell Sea and Shackleton's crew were left marooned 560 km from the nearest land. There were just three lifeboats to carry them all to safety, and Shackleton made the decision to have the sledging dogs and Mrs Chippy shot. Harry McNeish never forgave Shackleton for this.

The crew sailed on to the inhospitable Elephant Island in the lifeboats, and later a team led by Shackleton set off for the inhabited island of South Georgia. It was McNeish's carpentry skills that ensured their boat, the *James Caird*, could withstand the battering of some of the roughest seas in the world during its 1,300-km passage to South Georgia. All the crew members were rescued and survived.

Harry McNeish was denied the Polar Medal, despite his important contribution. It is thought that he had incurred Shackleton's wrath when he briefly rebelled while the men were moving camps on the sea ice. But in 2004, Harry McNeish and Mrs Chippy were remembered with the installation of a life-sized bronze statue of Mrs Chippy on McNeish's grave at Karori Cemetery in Wellington, New Zealand.

Mariska Wouters, chair of the Wellington branch of the New Zealand Antarctic Society, said of McNeish: 'We can't go back and give him a Polar Medal but this is one way of recognising what he contributed to the expedition.' Harry McNeish's grandson Tom McNeish believed that it was a fitting tribute to the carpenter and his much-loved cat. 'I think the cat was more important to him than the Polar Medal.'

FELIX

Felix was named after his point of entry into the UK at Felixstowe, after an epic journey from the Middle East…

RSPCA workers were astonished when they were called out to collect a bedraggled looking grey cat that had been found inside a shipping container filled with a delivery of sandpits and paddling pools in a depot near Coleshill,

Warwickshire. The container had been shipped all the way from Israel before being transferred to a train at Felixstowe and brought to the West Midlands.

Incredibly the cat, christened Felix, had been in the container all along. How he had survived the journey, which took seven weeks, without food was a bit of a mystery – it is thought that he gained some hydration by licking condensation from the walls of the container.

The little cat was emaciated and very distressed when he was discovered, but soon calmed down after he was moved from the Hams Hall Freight Depot to the RSPCA's animal hospital in Birmingham. The RSPCA pledged that they would foot the £800 quarantine bill temporarily while they looked for a suitable owner for the cat. RSPCA chief inspector Tim Scott said: 'He's such a plucky cat, it would be a shame for him not to have a new home waiting for him.'

Anyone who has lost a pet knows how difficult it can be to move on and accept that they're gone. When Gilly Delaney's cat Dixie went missing from her home in Erdington, Birmingham, Gilly was distraught, but she refused to give up hope of seeing her faithful companion again…

In 1999, Gilly Delaney's cat Dixie went missing. She was told that the cat had been killed by a car, and yet she couldn't give up hope of one day seeing her beloved pet again. Gilly put up posters, knocked on people's doors and contacted the local papers in the hope of finding Dixie – all to no avail. At one point, some years down the line, the couple were considering moving to Malta. But something held Gilly back – she couldn't shake off the hope that Dixie might return to the home that she once knew.

Nine years later, RSPCA officers turned up on Gilly's doorstep with a surprise for her – it was Dixie; bedraggled and somewhat worse for the wear, but instantly recognisable to Gilly as her long-lost pet. Incredibly, she had been found wandering the streets just half a mile from Gilly's home.

The RSPCA officers had been able to reunite the pet with her owner because she was microchipped – a quick scan of the chip allowed them to track Dixie's owner down and deliver her safely home. RSPCA Animal Collection Officer, Alan Pittaway, was delighted at the successful reunion and said: 'In 29 years of working for the RSPCA I have never seen anyone so excited and happy as Mrs Delaney.'

Dixie quickly settled back in to her life at home, and Gilly found that their bond was just as strong as ever. 'Dixie's personality, behaviour and little mannerisms have not changed at all,' Gilly explained. 'She is still a happy, contented cat who just wants to sit next to you on the sofa and have a fuss.' It was a happy ending for them both, and Dixie expressed her joy in a way that only cats can: 'She hasn't stopped purring since she came back through the door.'

Microchips: small but effective

Another cat, named Kofi, went missing for four years before being reunited with his owner Sarah Hawley. This cat was found a long way from home – Sarah had moved from Nottingham to Sheffield, and the cat was found 120 miles away in Ipswich. Because Sarah had had Kofi chipped and left her mother's details as an alternative point of contact, the RSPCA were able to reunite the pair.

A spokesperson for the RSPCA explained that 'Kofi would never have been identified if he had not been microchipped. The RSPCA takes in thousands of sick and injured cats every year. It is thought that many of these may have owners who never know what happened to their pet, because they had no identification.' The RSPCA now has a policy of microchipping all animals that it re-homes.

Microchipping is a short and painless procedure – a chip the size of a grain of rice is painlessly inserted under the animal's skin by injection. Once in, the microchip cannot move and is invisible from outside, but can be read a scanner and matched to the owners' details on the PetLog database. More than 450,000 pets have been microchipped in the last five years in the UK alone. And as these heart-warming stories show, getting your pet microchipped is definitely worth it.

EMILY

A young cat from Wisconsin called Emily wandered off one day, and was found three weeks later, 4,200 miles away from her home in France…

Donny and Lesley McElhiney from Appleton, Wisconsin, noticed that their cat Emily had gone missing in late September. Emily had run away before, so their first port of call was the local pet rescue centre. But when she didn't show up there, they didn't know where to look, and as time passed they began to give up hope of ever finding her. Three weeks later they were relieved when their vet called to tell them that Emily had been found – but they were surprised to learn that the little cat had made it as far away as France.

Emily was discovered by workers on 24 October at a paper lamination company near Nancy in France called Raflatac. She was inside a container of paper bales that had been sealed in Wisconsin and transported across America, then by ship across the Atlantic to Belgium, before making the final leg across land and into France. A spokesperson for Raflatac, Christèle Gozillon, was there when Emily was discovered. 'We received a container from Wisconsin full of bales of adhesive paper. We heard a cat meowing. It was a real surprise. We opened the container gently and a little, very frightened, cat ran and hid in the lorry engine,' she explained.

Christèle and her colleagues saw that the cat was wearing a tag with a name and address on it, so they contacted Emily's vet John Palarski, who in turn got in touch with the McElhineys. 'She has become the company mascot,' said Christèle. 'We call her Raflacat.'

It was quite an achievement for Emily to have survived her three-week journey. The McElhineys' vet thought she must have had access to some water and been able to catch mice on board the ship, but employees at Raflatac maintained that that there was nothing inside the sealed container except paper bales.

The story of *'Le chat Americain'*, as Emily became known in France, soon spread around the world, and was reported in the international media. The big question of the moment was: how would she get home to her family?

That's where Continental Airlines stepped in to give a helping hand. 'This was such a marvellous story, that we wanted to add something to it,' said Continental spokesman Philippe Fleury, speaking to AP Television News at Charles de Gaulle airport. Once the cat had cleared her one-month quarantine, she was escorted by cargo agent Gaylia McLeod from Paris to Newark in business class, then aboard a 50-seater from Newark to Milwaukee, where she was greeted by a huge crowd of reporters as she rejoined the McElhineys. 'I know it's close to the holidays,' a tearful McLeod said. 'I'm happy to be a part of reuniting Emily with her family.' McLeod had the honour of handing the intrepid voyager back to the McElhineys' son, nine-year-old Nick Herndon.

Emily meowed and pawed at reporters' microphones as the family told journalists about how happy they were to have Emily back safe and sound. 'She'll be held onto a lot all the way home. And then when we get home, too, she'll be cuddled a lot,' Donny McElhiney said. Nick thought that her trip over to the gastronomic centre of the world had done Emily some good. 'She's bigger and heavier than before,' he said.

Windy takes to the skies

Wing Commander Guy Penrose Gibson VC led the 'Dam Busters' raid in 1943, successfully destroying two large dams in the Ruhr area of Germany. His pet cat Windy is said to have accompanied him on many dangerous wartime airborne missions. The plucky cat, that also knew how to swim, is said to have put in 'more flying hours than most cats'.

MIMINE

Cats seem to have a knack of returning to their old homes, even when they've moved with their families hundreds of miles away. But when their owners leave without them and they manage to track them down, as Mimine did, it is rather more mysterious...

Mimine was given away to another family by her French owners in March 2006 when they decided to move away from their home in Toulouse in the south of France. They were going to settle in Tréveray in the Lorraine region, so they didn't expect to see their pet again.

But 13 months later, in April 2007, the brown-and-grey-striped cat turned up unexpectedly on the doorstep of the family's new home. The children, aged six and eight, recognised their long-lost furry friend immediately. They couldn't believe their eyes. Though the cat wasn't microchipped or wearing a collar, her unique markings along with her particular disdain for croquettes convinced the family that it was indeed their old cat come to find them.

Vet Marie-Pierre Francois said: 'We have verified that the journey definitely took place.' The three-year-old cat would have had to cover just over a mile a day during her 13 months on the road, covering a distance of around 500 miles. Mimine seemed to be in good shape, though she did have some blisters on her paws and a few ticks she'd picked up along the way to show for her epic journey.

Marie-Pierre said that she didn't think the family would be giving up their pet again. 'I'm pretty sure her old family will now be keeping her for good. She's certainly proved her loyalty.' How Mimine managed to track down her family will remain a mystery.

ONE OF A KIND

And then there are the cats that defy all belief. The cats in this section truly are wonder cats. Whether they have a unique ability, a bizarre habit or a rare physical quality, each of these felines has managed to astound us, and to make us realise that as long as cats are around, there will never be a dull moment.

NORA

Piano instructor Betsy Alexander from Philadelphia has an unusual pianist that sometimes plays in her studio: her grey tabby cat Nora…

Betsy Alexander adopted Nora from a rescue centre in Cherry Hill, New Jersey. She is named after the artist Leonora Carrington, and has certainly proved to have her own creative tendencies. As Betsy is a piano instructor she spends a lot of time in her studio teaching, and Nora seemed to show an interest in the piano straight away, sometimes dancing in circles on top of the piano while Betsy played. When she was one year old she climbed up on the bench in front of a Yamaha Disklavier piano and, to Betsy's amazement, began to press the keys with her paws. After that she began to regularly play the piano side by side with Betsy, who has two of the instruments lined up in her teaching studio.

With some encouragement from her students, Betsy made a film of Nora playing the piano and posted it on the website YouTube in 2007. The response was phenomenal. The video received 17 million hits and attracted the attention of the media – soon the clip was being shown on VH1, Conan O'Brien, Tyra Banks, Ellen, Martha Stewart, and many more; there was even a live performance by Nora on *The Today Show* that proved the YouTube clip was not fabricated but a genuine record of this cat's extraordinary talent. 'This is her own thing; it's not a trick,' said owner Betsy. 'It's not something we taught her.'

Though Nora seems to enjoy the attention she gets from playing the piano, her owner Betsy says she does it to please herself: 'She plays when we're not in the room; she plays when we're in the room; sometimes she plays when we don't want her to play. I can be teaching a child or an adult who is trying to concentrate and then Nora hops on the bench.'

Nora 'The Piano Cat' has received well-wishes from the Piano Man himself, Billy Joel. There is a website dedicated to her, where she has her own blog. She also has her own DVD, a book called *Nora the Piano Cat's Guide to Becoming a Good Musician* has been published, and a CD has been released that features a track that incorporates her playing.

CHARLIE

Hannah Smith of Denny, Falkirk, has a pet that doesn't like to hang around the front door waiting to be let in like your average cat; daredevil Charlie has found his own ingenious way of coming and going at will…

Hannah Smith got Charlie as a kitten. 'Out of the litter he was the one that looked most mischievous and I liked that about him,' she said. Well, he certainly lived up to her expectations.

Hannah lives in a block of flats in Denny, Falkirk. The entrance to the building is through a shared front door, but one day Charlie got tired of waiting there for someone to let him in after he'd nipped out for some air. Instead he decided to scale the 13-foot roughcast wall at the rear of the building and hop onto the balcony of Hannah's flat on the first floor and meow loudly until the flat door was opened. This became a regular habit for Charlie, nicknamed 'Spider-cat' by Hannah, and the cause of much amusement in the neighbourhood.

Of course, most cats are good climbers, but their talents usually stop at scaling the nearest tree in search of a safe resting place or vantage point. Beth Skillings, clinical veterinary officer for the charity Cats Protection, was impressed by Charlie's outstanding abilities. 'It's unusual to see a cat scaling such a high wall. He must have very strong claws.'

Hannah's two other pet cats seem to have no inclination to follow in Charlie's footsteps – they prefer to watch from the balcony as their fellow feline performs his daily death-defying feat.

MIDGE

When Martin Humphreys from Wrose, Yorkshire, adopted a one-eyed cat named Midge, he had no idea she'd turn out to have a unique quality that would see the pair shooting to stardom…

Parish councillor Martyn Humphreys, who lives in the Yorkshire village of Wrose, adopted Midge as a kitten from a rescue centre in Bradford. At the time she still had both eyes, but one was severely damaged and before he could bring her home she had to undergo an operation to have it removed. Martyn described her as a spirited cat, and said that her disability seemed to make her all the more popular with local children.

It wasn't long before the energetic cat began accompanying him on trips to the local shop. She would follow him there, wait for him on the wall outside and then follow along the road home. Sometimes the cat would run for the return journey and one day Martyn decided to run too, but something extraordinary happened. No matter how fast Martyn ran, the little cat ran faster – she just wouldn't let him overtake. He thought it might have been a one off, but on their next visit to the shop he tried again, only to be beaten to his front door once more. It soon became a common sight in the village to see Martyn racing his cat home, but the one-eyed cat would never let him win.

But it doesn't end there. Martyn knew that their story was special – he'd certainly never heard of a one-eyed racing cat from Yorkshire before! And so when he won £1,000 in a contest at work he decided to use the money to make a short film about his very own wonder cat, Midge. Martyn made *The Great Race*, as the short film was named, with Leeds producers Motus TV and wrote the soundtrack, performed by a local children's choir, himself. To his delight, the film was shown at the Shorter Film Corner at the Cannes Film Festival 2009. In the film, Martyn and Midge race down the road. Before they set off Martyn, a true sportsman, shakes Midge's paw and says: 'It's you against me, man against cat, and may the best life form win.'

Martyn had hopes to get one of the big film studios like Walt Disney or Twentieth Century Fox onboard and make Midge's story into what he said would be 'one of the greatest children's films of all time'. Later in 2009 Midge made a guest appearance on ITV 1's *Animals Do The Funniest Things*, billed as 'one of the most unique cats in the world'. Perhaps we haven't heard the last of Midge yet...

FRANKIE

Julie Bishop from Swindon was somewhat alarmed and a little embarrassed to discover that her cat Frankie had developed a rather naughty habit...

Julie Bishop, 52, lived with her partner Gary Witts, 47, in Swindon. They got Frankie from a farm in Wiltshire in 2006. The two-year-old cat proved to be a very independent individual; though he was friendly and liked to sleep on his owner's shoulder, he would also make it clear when he was in no mood for cuddles, and enjoyed the freedom of coming and going through his cat flap at all hours.

Then Frankie began to bring things home with him from his trips outdoors – soft toys that he'd cunningly swiped from other houses in the neighbourhood. He would drag each one through the cat flap and drop it in the same spot in the lounge. 'They're all soft toys for cats I think,' said Julie, 'About fifteen of them are all the same leopard.' But Frankie didn't seem to show much interest in his booty once he'd got it home. 'He doesn't really play with them. He dumps them down and goes out looking for something else.'

Whatever the cat burglar's motivation for his thieving sprees, he certainly seemed to have a rare talent for getting away with it – in the space of a year he had pilfered around thirty-five cuddly toys. The collection included teddy bears, leopards and a giant squeaky beefburger. There were also some less savoury items that Julie discovered deposited on her living room floor: two green witches' heads on Halloween, old socks, nappy sacks, half-eaten beefburgers and chips, and the more traditional dead mice and birds. Could this be the first recorded case of feline kleptomania?

Though Julie acknowledged that Frankie's career of crime was progressing at an impressive rate, she has put up posters around her neighbourhood in the hope of tracing the rightful owners of the miscreant feline's swag.

FLOOK

To receive a telegram from the Queen is a very great honour indeed. So when one arrived addressed to Chris Evans' cat Flook, you can imagine how surprised and delighted he was…

Chris Evans from Windermere, Cumbria, got his Burmese cat Flook when she was just a little kitten and was very proud when she made it to the grand old age of 100 in cat years (about 23 in human years).

So proud was he, in fact, that he wrote a letter to the Queen to tell her that his much-loved pet had reached a cat century. Now, normally the Queen only writes to *humans* to recognise their reaching 100 years, but in this case it appears she was moved to break with tradition, because some time later an official congratulatory telegram signed by Her Majesty landed on Chris's doormat.

'I really just sent the letter tongue in cheek and didn't expect anything back,' said Chris. 'But when I got the letter from Buckingham Palace I nearly fell over.' As the first cat on record to have been honoured in this way, Flook is pretty special.

Living to a ripe old age

At just six months of age cats reach adolescence, and by the time they are a year old are considered to be fully grown adults. This accelerated speed of development then slows down, however; by around the nine/ten year mark they are middle-aged, and those that reach their twenties are regarded as centenarians in human terms.

The life expectancy of domestic cats used to be between 12 to 15 years, but improved diet and veterinary care have increased this over time, so that it is not unusual for a healthy cat to live to 16–20 years. Mixed breed cats tend to live longer than their pedigree counterparts, and females are likely to outlive males by around two years. Cats that have been neutered or spayed also seem to have a longer life expectancy than those that have not, which could be down to them living life at a calmer pace, without the wear and tear of parenthood or territorial battles.

EDDIE

A vet who was carrying out routine vaccinations on a set of four kittens was surprised to discover that one of them was a very rare marvel of nature…

Karen Horne ran a veterinary surgery in Harpenden, Herts. One day a family of four eight-week-old tortoiseshell kittens were brought in for vaccination by local charity Cat and Kitten Rescue. As Karen made her examination she was amazed to discover that one of the cats was a male. This was totally unexpected because cats with tortoiseshell colouring are always female – it shouldn't be genetically possible for a male tortoiseshell to exist.

Because male cats, just like male human beings, only have one X chromosome in their DNA, it is technically unfeasible for them to inherit different colours – but on rare occasions it does happen. The odds are 400,000 to one, making it an extremely uncommon accident.

Karen, who adopted the cat, named him Eddie, after the cross-dressing comic Eddie Izzard because, she said, 'he is essentially a boy dressed in girls' clothing'. She already had a pretty full family of five cats, four dogs and three children, but couldn't resist taking Eddie in because he was such a rare fluke of nature. 'My colleagues and I have 30 years of experience between us and we have never seen anything like this,' she explained. 'I feel like the luckiest vet ever just to see a tortie tomcat, and even luckier to have him live with me.'

Karen felt confident that there were no signs of gender confusion in Eddie, and though in theory he should be infertile because of his genetic make-up she planned to have him neutered when he reached puberty anyway, just like any other household tomcat.

UNNAMED CAT

A fluffy white cat in Chongqing, China, became the centre of attention when it underwent an astonishing physical transformation…

Owners of a fluffy white cat in Chongqing, China, were receiving lots of visitors who all wanted to see their pet cat when they heard the news that he had grown a pair of wings.

Two wing-shaped appendages sprouted from the back of the little cat when he was just one year old. His owners said that cat was doing just fine and didn't seem at all bothered by the growths – in fact, he seemed to be enjoying all the attention.

What would happen next – would the winged cat take to skies? Luckily for the local bird population, the cat wasn't set to develop the gift of flight. His 'wings' were thought to be the result of a very rare genetic condition in cats known as feline cutaneous asthenia which makes the cat's skin exceptionally stretchy, or hyperextensible. Grooming or rubbing against hard surfaces can lead to the skin being kneaded out, as seen in the Chongqing cat.

Though rare, there have been other cats documented in history, most famous perhaps being the Manchester winged cat which lived in Trafford Park for some years. Photographs were published in the *Manchester Evening*

News and caused a fair bit of controversy. In *Dr Shuker's Casebook: In Pursuit of Marvels and Mysteries*, Karl Shuker presents a comprehensive collection of case studies of these extraordinary animals.

DANTE

Becky Page from Tasburgh, Norfolk, already had three chickens, a rabbit, two guinea pigs, a rat, a hamster and fish, but when she found an abandoned and starving kitten she just had to take the poor creature home. But then she discovered that Dante, as she named him, had some rather peculiar dietary requirements…

Becky Page first met Dante in an alleyway. The little black and white kitten was starving and emaciated, so she took him back to her home in Tasburgh, near Norwich, to give him some food. She prepared him a big bowl of chicken, but to her surprise the hungry cat turned his nose up at it. Determined to get him to eat, Becky tried again with a plate of fish – still no luck. As she wondered what to try next, the kitten wandered over to the kitchen bin where some leftover vegetables lay on the floor. Quick as a flash he gobbled them hungrily down – and Becky has never seen him eat meat since. In fact, he may well be the world's first vegetarian cat.

Becky, a child minder aged 21, said: 'Since he had that first plate of veg, he won't go near anything fatty and prefers the things I grow in the garden.' So what does this cat that shuns tinned cat food feed on? He enjoys fresh fruit and veg from his owner's garden, like Brussels sprouts and rhubarb, and melon and asparagus also seem to tickle his taste buds. Becky has even caught him raiding the fruit bowl for bananas on a few occasions.

Director of veterinary services at Cats Protection Maggie Roberts commented: 'This is extremely rare, I have never before heard of a cat that will not eat meat. We advise that cats be fed a complete cat food, which provides all of the necessary nutrients in the right balance.' Dante's choice of diet is extraordinary because cats are natural carnivores; there are certain vital nutrients that they can only get in sufficient quantities from meat. Although dogs can survive on a vegetarian diet, cats are more specialised. They can only get taurine, an amino acid essential for cats, by eating meat – a prolonged lack of this substance causes a cat's retina to slowly degenerate, meaning it could eventually become irreversibly blind. They also need to eat meat for arachidonic acid – this fatty acid helps wounds to heal.

So, in theory, picky eater Dante shouldn't be able to survive on his diet, but he appears to be as fit as any cat his age. This could be down to his owner's sneaky ploys to get him to eat a balanced diet. 'I have to smuggle bits of meat in among the veggies because I want him to get all the nutrients he needs. But sometimes he spots the meat and will just leave it.'

Becky is convinced that the gentle cat is not only vegetarian, but has no interest in hunting either. He's a shy cat that doesn't like to venture outside very much. 'I've never seen him chase any birds or small animals,' she says. 'He hunts bits of string around the house instead to fulfil his predatory instincts.' Neither does he seem to show any interest in Becky's collection of other pets, which includes chickens, a rabbit, guinea pigs, a rat, a hamster and fish – creatures that would have most cats licking their lips in anticipation!

YODA

Valerie and Ted Rock from Chicago had just lost a cat that had been with them for 20 years and thought they would never have a pet again. That was until they saw a cat so unusual they couldn't resist bringing him home with them…

Valerie and Ted Rock, both in their sixties, were out for a drink with friends in a bar near their home in the Chicago suburb of Downer's Grove one night when they saw a peculiar looking cat being passed around by drinkers that were very curious about his appearance, and not surprisingly – the kitten had four ears!

The unusual cat was part of a large litter and the owners were looking for a home for him. The couple immediately fell for the four-eared feline when he was passed to Ted and promptly cuddled up in the crook of his neck and fell asleep. They asked the owner if they could adopt him and named him Yoda, after the diminutive Jedi knight of *Star Wars* fame. Apparently George Lucas based the character on his own pet cat.

Yoda has a normal set of ears and two extra flaps situated just behind that cannot detect sound. One of the first things Valerie did was to get the eight-week-old kitten checked out by her local vet. The cat was found to be completely healthy and his hearing was perfectly normal – in every way he was an ordinary cat apart from his extra set of ears, and the vet just didn't know what to make of those. 'We have spoken with other vets in our acquaintance, and they likewise had never encountered anything like this,' said Valerie.

The couple then began to realise just how special Yoda really was. 'As a result, he has been an indoor cat and has a chip installed in case he gets lost,' Valerie explained. 'Yoda is so different that we were concerned that he might be catnapped.' The couple enjoy showing their unusual cat off, but some people have asked them if they purposefully had his ears cut to look the way he does.

Valerie described Yoda as a perfectly normal, affectionate, curious cat and said he was a joy to have around because he is so much more sociable than others cats she has known. Strangely, he doesn't have an audible purr, and when he meows it is very soft. And he does have one other quirky attribute, said Valerie: 'He does have an interesting obsession with bread – I can't leave bread on the counter for a moment.'

Hemingway cats

Polydactyl cats have more than the usual number of toes on their paws due to a genetic mutation. Nobel-prize-winning author Ernest Hemingway was a famous lover of these cats – he had been given a six-toed cat by a ship's captain, and he eventually had quite a collection of them. When he died in 1961, his former home in Key West, Florida, became a museum and a home for his cats. It currently houses about fifty descendants of his favoured felines, about half of which are polydactyl. Because of his love for these animals, Hemingway cat, or simply Hemingway, is a slang term which has come to be used to refer to them.

LIL'BIT

A woman from Arizona discovered that a little bit of love can go a long way when she was told that one of her cat's litter of kittens wouldn't survive…

A 47-year-old woman from Arizona was delighted when her cat Lil'Pine gave birth to five kittens – three male and two female – under her computer table. But one of the male kittens, named Lil'Bit (short for 'a little bit of love') was very different to normal cats. 'When I picked Lil'Bit up I suddenly spotted that he had two faces. I was so shocked that I nearly dropped him,' said his owner.

Lil'Bit had been born with two mouths, two noses and four eyes, the middle pair almost merging, but just one pair of ears. The woman was concerned for the kitten and phoned the kitten rescue service for advice. They warned her that he probably wouldn't survive, but she didn't want to give up on him just yet. 'I didn't see why he shouldn't be given the chance to live,' she explained. 'Everything is possible.' So she set about the task of bringing the little kitten up. She got him a heating pad to keep him warm and fed him every 15 minutes from a pipette on baby milk, and kept this up for two or three months before introducing him to proper cat food. As the kitten had difficulty walking, using the litter tray was a bit of a problem, but she found that premature baby nappies seemed to do the trick. Lil'Bit was soon thriving and looked all set to live to a ripe old age.

Vets that have examined the cat say he is a medical marvel, and believe he may in fact have two brains: one face can go to sleep while the other remains awake, and if he gets a cold, the nose on only one of the faces will run. 'I have also seen him sneeze out of one side and not the other and blink on one side of his face but not the other,' said his owner. 'And when he purrs it is like he is purring in stereo.'

Lil'Bit has received quite a bit of attention from the media because he really is a unique cat, but his owner has chosen to remain anonymous because she doesn't want any unwanted visitors turning up at her house to see the cat, as she believes this could be very stressful for him and make him ill. She also hasn't put Lil'Bit in for any X-rays or operations because she'd rather not upset him – but with a little bit of love and lots of care he seemed to be doing fine anyway. The mother of two boys added: 'The whole family loves Lil'Bit.'

NICOLASA

Inquisitive cats like to watch what their owners do and get involved – unravelling the wool while their owner knits, or swatting the keyboard as their owner tries to type. But Nicolasa, a cat from Peru, took curiosity to the extreme when she hopped on her owner's surf board…

Nicolasa is the world's one and only surfing cat. This unlikely pastime – given that cats are supposed to loathe water – was discovered one day when owner Domingo Pianezzi, of Lima, Peru, was down at the San Bartolo beach with his pet cat and the fearless moggy hopped on to his board for a ride.

He claims that the little tortoiseshell cat enjoys catching a wave more than catching mice. Maybe the little cat even has it in her to turn pro – hanging on with her claws hooked around the front of the board, she certainly doesn't look in danger of falling off as her owner rides smiling behind.

Video footage of the pair out surfing posted on the website YouTube has sparked some speculation over whether the cat is actually enjoying herself, but she doesn't seem any worse the wear for the experience. At the end of the clip she looks like she's done for the day; she slips off the board and swims towards the shore where she is scooped out of the shallows by a waiting friend, wrapped in a towel and given a loving cuddle.

Performing cats

Unlike dogs, cats aren't thought of as being receptive to being trained to perform tricks. However, there have been some rather astonishing exceptions to this rule.

In 1829, Signor Cappelli's performing musical cats were billed as 'the greatest wonder in England'. These talented felines wowed audiences with their trapeze and juggling skills, along with rather more practical talents such as grinding rice, roasting coffee and turning a spit to draw water out of a well. Yuri Kouklachev of the Moscow State Circus trained a troupe of cats to jump over obstacles, do handstands and even play chess. He found success by training the animals at night, when he claimed they were more receptive because of their nocturnal nature.

Cats are in fact much better than dogs at learning tricks by themselves, because they observe very carefully. For example, many cats quickly learn how to jump at a door and open it by pulling down the handle, just by watching humans. They are very quick to notice which of their actions attract their human's attention; usually this is used to manipulate their human – say, by scratching at furniture when they want to go out – but this capacity to learn can be transformed into astounding tricks by a patient trainer who is willing to let the cat learn on its own terms.

OSCAR

Oscar, a fluffy, grey-and-white-brindled cat adopted by a nursing home in Providence, Rhode Island, is often to be seen pacing the corridors – and he seems to possess a rather unusual ability…

In July 2005, the dementia unit of the Steere House Nursing and Rehabilitation Centre in Providence, Rhode Island, adopted a kitten and named him Oscar, after a well-known American hot dog brand. The centre treats people with Alzheimer's, Parkinson's disease and other illnesses of old age. The little cat seemed quite at home there, and after six months the doctors and nurses noticed that Oscar was making his own rounds, sniffing around patients and observing them carefully.

However, Oscar was not generally friendly to the patients and was selective about who he visited – in fact, staff soon noticed a pattern. Sometimes he would just sniff the patients and turn away, but on other occasions he would curl up next to them on the bed. The patients he stayed with would pass away within a few hours. Was he somehow able to predict when patients were about to die? Dr Joan Teno, a member of staff at the home, was convinced that he had a rare talent when he made his thirteenth correct prediction. The patient in question had taken a turn for the worse – she had stopped eating, had difficulty breathing and there was a bluish tinge to her legs; all signs that can mean death is imminent. But Oscar didn't seem to be concerned, and didn't stick around in the room. Dr Teno, who was convinced that the patient didn't have long to live, began to think that Oscar's 'predictions' up until that point had been coincidence – but then ten hours later, Oscar appeared at the woman's bedside. She was dead within two hours, proving that Oscar's skill was much more precise than the medical staff's.

By the time he was two years old Oscar had predicted the deaths of 25 residents, and staff began alerting the families of patients he curled up next to, so that they would have time to visit their loved one before the end. Rather than seeing the cat as a harbinger of death, many families seem thankful for his presence and the early warning that he provides. 'They appreciate the companionship that the cat provides for their dying loved ones,' says Dr David Dosa, a geriatrician at Rhode Island who also visits patients at Steere House. 'It may be half a day, sometimes two, three, four hours, but he's always there when the patient dies.' Indeed, even after a patient has passed away, Oscar remains with the body until the undertaker arrives and attends the funeral procession to the door, watching over them as they leave the building. There has only been one death in the home he wasn't present for – and that is because the family of the patient refused to allow him in the room. He remained outside the door, pacing up and down and meowing; eventually he had to be removed from the unit because of the fuss he was making.

Oscar has been the subject of a study published in the *New England Journal of Medicine*. David Dosa was involved in the research and said that Oscar 'seems to understand when patients are about to die'. But how is he able to do this? One suggestion is that he notices a change in staff behaviour towards patients whose health is deteriorating – but that doesn't explain the cases where staff were not concerned about a patient, and yet Oscar's arrival at their bed preceded their death by two hours. Having grown up in a nursing home he may have become more attuned to the various signs of oncoming death – but then the other cat that lives on the premises has never exhibited such abilities. Some believe that Oscar acts as a familiar and is in psychic contact with the patients in their final hours, but it is far more likely that he has learnt to recognise certain scents created by chemical and hormonal changes in the body that are imperceptible to humans and signal the approach of death. Certainly, research has shown that some cats and dogs are able to identify the presence of cancer in humans, and to predict seizures. His reasons for staying at a patient's side once he has predicted they are about to die cannot be explained by this theory, however; perhaps he feels an urge to comfort them as they leave this world. Dr Teno said: 'He's not a bad omen. He comforts the dying patients – and what's striking is that, in a centre that offers a real gold-standard in end-of-life treatment, Oscar seems to be mimicking the behaviour of those who work there. He makes the room feel like more of a homely setting, and has become part of the soothing ritual.'

A wall plaque was put up in the home in recognition of Oscar's 'compassionate hospice care'. His story has been widely reported in the media, and the publicity has resulted in a surge of letters and emails to Steere House from people claiming to know of other cats with similar abilities.

USEFUL RESOURCES AND INFORMATION

Battersea Dogs and Cats Home

Battersea Dogs and Cats Home has been caring for and reuniting lost pets with their owners for over 150 years and boasts a dedicated Behavioural Unit to help ensure that any new arrivals can be introduced to their new owners successfully.
Website: www.battersea.org.uk

Cat Chat – The Cat Rescue Resource

Cat Chat is a registered web-based charity which works with other existing organisations to find permanent homes for unwanted and abandoned felines. Their 'Virtual Cat Shelters' provide all the necessary adoption information and help to re-home over 5,000 cats a year.
Website: www.catchat.org

Cat Register and Rescue

This Falkirk-based rescue group works mainly with sick or injured stray and feral cats, caring for them until they can be returned to a safe site or re-homed. This charity

strongly adopts an attitude of preservation towards these less-fortunate animals.
Website: www.rainbowsedge.co.uk

Cats Protection

Cats Protection is the UK's leading cat welfare charity and helps over 193,000 unwanted cats and kittens through a national network of 253 volunteer-run branches and 29 adoption centres. The charity's vision is a world where every cat is treated with kindness and an understanding of its needs.
National Helpline: 03000 12 12 12
Website: www.cats.org.uk
Email: helpline@cats.org.uk

Celia Hammond Animal Trust

Founded in 1986, born out of Celia's personal concerns about the rising feral cat population, this award-winning organisation has been responsible for establishing two dedicated clinics in London offering vaccinations and neutering at a low cost. Celia has also set up a cat sanctuary in East Sussex to care for cats awaiting a new home.
Website: www.celiahammond.org

Crafty Cat

Crafty Cat Behaviour and Feline Psychology Forum is an impressive online resource for owners concerned about their pet's behaviour. Here you will find an extensive behaviour reference library giving details of various types of behaviour and what they most likely signify.
Website: www.craftycat.co.uk

Feline Advisory Bureau

An organisation focused on advancing knowledge and understanding of cats in both private and public sectors, helping fund veterinary research and cattery training schemes as well as holding regular meetings and conferences, most of which are open to the public.
Website: www.fabcats.org

Kitty Mania

A useful site for those looking for information on particular breeds of cat available in the UK, along with a searchable directory giving details of where to find particular breeders in your area.
Website: www.kittymania.co.uk

Moggies – Home of the Online Cat Guide

Offers an amusing and informative collection of all things feline; from poems to jokes, breed information to famous quotes, you are bound to find something of interest here.
Website: www.moggies.co.uk

Pets As Therapy (PAT)

Pets As Therapy, or PAT for short, is a registered charity that provides therapeutic visits to all kinds of health establishments by volunteers with their own friendly, temperament-tested cats and dogs. The charity operates on the premise that, while research on the proven medical benefits of the company of cats and dogs is still developing, there is no doubt that many sick or ailing individuals appreciate the warm company of a furry feline

or canine companion. All PAT dogs and cats are certified by accredited assessors and given the necessary checks by qualified vets before being permitted to make any visits.
Telephone: 01844 345 445
Website: www.petsastherapy.org

PDSA

Founded by Maria Dickin in 1917, the People's Dispensary for Sick Animals provides more than 2 million free veterinary treatments each year, funded completely by public support.
Website: www.pdsa.org.uk
Telephone: 0800 731 2502

Purina: Cats

As well as being experts in cat nutrition, the team at Purina have plenty of reliable and professional advice to offer about the health and happiness of your cat online at their website, which has a collection of articles on a range of useful subjects.
Website: www.purina.com/cats

Purr 'n' Fur UK

A long-standing website offering a wide selection of information and articles for cat lovers, featuring book reviews, real-life accounts of some remarkable moggies, and a fascinating collection of entries on famous felines through history.
Website: www.purr-n-fur.org.uk

Scottish SPCA

The Scottish Society for the Prevention of Cruelty to Animals is Scotland's animal welfare charity, rescuing, rehabilitating and re-homing wild and domestic animals in need.
Website: www.scottishspca.org
Animal Helpline: 03000 999 999

StartACattery

This site is an excellent resource for anyone wanting to get involved and start their own cattery. Here you will find expert advice on all aspects of this endeavour, including everything from selecting a suitable business site, to promotion and obtaining a licence.
Website: www.startacattery.co.uk

The Cat Site

Offers an impressive range of online forums covering practically everything relating to cats and their well-being.
Website: www.thecatsite.com

The Governing Council of the Cat Fancy

The GCCF is the primary governing body of the Cat Fancy in the UK, which is essentially the feline equivalent of the Kennel Club. Similarly, they are interested in the appreciation and promotion of fine-bred domestic animals, to which end they host an annual 'Supreme Show' which features exhibitions and prize-giving. The GCCF also has its own charity, The Cat Welfare Trust, which helps to invest funds into a range of activities to benefit cats.
Website: www.gccfcats.org

The National Cat Club

The UK's oldest cat club was founded in 1887 and holds an annual national show for members to celebrate their cats and be commended on their efforts in preserving fine breeding standards.

Website: www.nationalcatclub.co.uk

Do you have your own wonder cat story?

If you have your own stories of amazing feline behaviour, we'd love to read them. Please send them to us at the address below and we'll include the best in any new edition of this book:

Ashley Morgan
c/o Summersdale Publishers Ltd
46 West Street
Chichester
West Sussex
PO19 1RP

DOG HEROES

True Stories of Canine Courage

Ben Holt

ISBN: 978-1-84024-767-1 Paperback £7.99

- Swansea Jack, the Labrador that rescued 27 people from drowning
- Max, the collie cross that warned his owner that she had breast cancer
- Shadow, the Rottweiler that saved three young children from a pair of hungry wolves

These are just a few of the inspiring true stories in this collection of dog tales from around the world. Included are some astonishing first-hand accounts by people who have witnessed quick-thinking and resourceful dogs in action.

From trained lifeguard dogs and guide dogs to loyal family pets and unnamed strays, each of these courageous canines has shown true heroism – sometimes in the most surprising of ways. Heart-melting, dramatic and often deeply moving, *Dog Heroes* proves why dogs can save and change lives, and are truly our best friends.

'*Selection of true tales from around the world of canine courage...*'
YOUR DOG magazine

'*some of the most astonishing, fascinating and heart-warming stories of dogs' heroic acts*'
IRISH NEWS

CATS IN THE BELFRY

'The most enchanting cat book ever'
Jilly Cooper

DOREEN TOVEY

CATS IN THE BELFRY

Doreen Tovey

ISBN: 978-1-84024-452-6 Paperback £6.99

'*It wasn't, we discovered as the months went by, that Sugieh was particularly wicked. It was just that she was a Siamese.*'

Animal lover Doreen and her husband Charles acquire their first Siamese kitten to rid themselves of an invasion of mice. But Sugieh is not just any cat. She's an actress, a prima donna, an iron hand in a delicate, blue-pointed glove. She quickly establishes herself as queen of the house, causing chaos daily by screaming like a banshee, chewing up telegrams, and tearing holes in anything made of wool.

First published over forty years ago, this warm and witty classic tale is a truly enjoyable read for anyone who's ever been owned by a cat.

'*If there is a funnier book about cats I for one do not want to read it. I would hurt myself laughing, might even die of laughter*'

THE SCOTSMAN

'*Every so often, there comes along a book – or if you're lucky books – which gladden the heart, cheer the soul... Just such books are those written by Doreen Tovey*' CAT WORLD